CONTENTS

KEY TO AT A GLANCE TABLES

SOWING/PLANTING   FLOWERING

At a glance tables are your quick guide.
For full information, consult the accompanying text.

---

*LEFT: Mixing perennials with annuals ensures a summer long
outpouring of bloom. Here, white spires of Lysimachia ephemerum
rub shoulders with yellow coreopsis and annual pink lavatera,
phlox and everlasting flowers.*

GROWING PERENNIALS

Many of the loveliest and best-loved flowering plants are perennials. Like annuals, perennials provide a colourful display, but they have the advantage that they don't need to be changed at least twice a year. Perennials are easy-care plants which have a major place in low maintenance gardens.

Perennials remain alive for a number of years, unlike annuals which usually last only one season, and biennials which grow and flower through a second season or year. Perennials form a variable group in terms of their size and foliage, flower shape, style and colour. In fact, there is a perennial to suit almost every climate, aspect and soil, and some can even be grown in containers. Perennials can also be planted among shrubs, to form a background for bulbs or annuals, or in their own separate areas. Perennial borders make lively, exciting features.

ABOVE: The white form of the purple coneflower showing its attractive, recurved petals.

LEFT: A tender, bright pink argyranthemum, and scabious, in the foreground add perennial interest to this colourful, mixed border featuring soft hues offset by green.

PERENNIALS COMBINE with annuals to form a free-flowing, rich, colourful border, a highlight of mid-summer in this gorgeous cottage garden. A pink shrub rose is flanked by two varieties of aster, while deep blue delphiniums add scale and height at the back.

EVERGREEN OR HERBACEOUS?

Some perennials are evergreen but many are herbaceous. Most herbaceous perennials grow rapidly during spring and summer to flower during the summer and autumn. After flowering they gradually die back to the crown or fleshy roots, and they remain dormant during cold winters. Since most of the hardy herbaceous perennials come from climates with very severe, cold winters they die down naturally in the autumn. In warmer areas, where they do not become completely dormant and some growth continues year round, the plants do not live as long. However, it is simple to renew these perennials as division is easy, and most increase rapidly. In time, a few can even become invasive.

PLANTING PERENNIALS

Soil preparation

Because perennials are long-term plants and because they are close planted, good soil preparation is essential. Although some perennials, such as astilbes and hostas, enjoy damp soil, many prefer well-drained conditions. If you are planting any of the latter group, check your drainage before planting. Dig some holes in the bed, fill them with water and see how long

PERENNIALS FOR SUN AND SHADE

SUNNY BORDERS

- Agapanthus
- Delphinium
- Diascia
- Eryngium
- Gypsophila
- Helenium
- Hemerocallis
- Miscanthus
- Oenothera
- Papaver
- Sedum
- Stachys

SHADY BORDERS

- *Alchemilla mollis*
- Aquilegia
- Bergenia
- Candelabra primula
- Digitalis
- Epimedium
- *Gunnera manicata*
- Helleborus
- Hosta
- Polygonatum
- Primula
- Pulmonaria
- Rodgersia (dappled)

PURE WHITE shasta daisies light up the summer garden, putting on a strong display from early summer to early autumn.

it takes to drain away. If there is still water in the holes 12 hours later, you will need to improve the drainage by installing a system of sub-soil drains.

If the soil is very heavy clay, which remains wet but not waterlogged for a long time, you should dig in some gypsum, about 300g per sq m (10.5oz per sq yd). Digging in large quantities of decayed manure or compost a few weeks before planting will also improve clay soils, and it is a must in sandy soils that have poor moisture and nutrient retention.

Thorough weeding of the area is essential, too, as it is difficult to remove weeds in densely planted beds. Remove the weeds you can see, dig or fork over the area again, water and wait for the next lot of weeds to emerge. You may need to repeat this step if the area has been neglected for any length of time. Hand weeding or spraying with glyphosate should eliminate most weeds, but you will need to be persistent to control oxalis, bindweed and ground elder. This sounds like a lot of work when you are eager to plant out your garden, but it will be worth the wait and the effort in the long run.

Planting perennials from containers

Garden centres and nurseries will stock some perennials, especially when they are in flower. These can be planted in the garden like any other container-grown plant. When the plant is removed from its pot, loosen the rootball a little so that the roots can extend into the surrounding soil. It is essential that the planting hole is about twice the width of the container and approximately the same depth. The soil level around the plant should be exactly the same as it was in the container. Give a thorough soaking after planting. Also apply a deep mulch to the soil around the plant.

Planting bare-rooted perennials

There are also nurseries that specialise in perennials. These nurseries usually advertise in popular gardening magazines, have detailed catalogues with thorough plant descriptions, and sell by mail-order. Plants are delivered during their dormant season, which for the majority is from late autumn

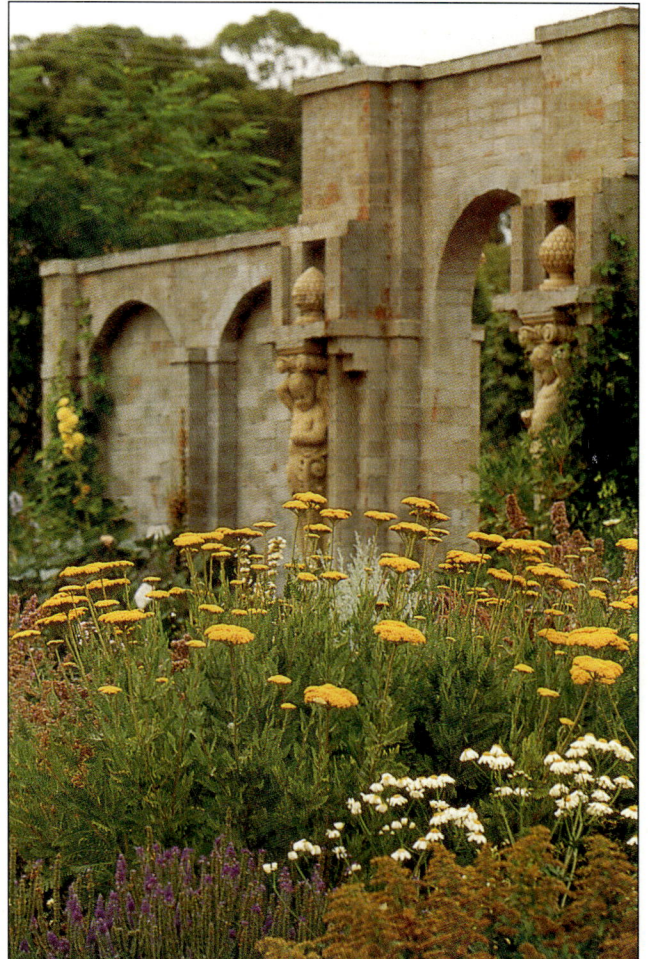

A HIGH STONE WALL marks the boundary of this meadow garden filled with golden fern-leaf yarrow, daisies and purple loosestrife.

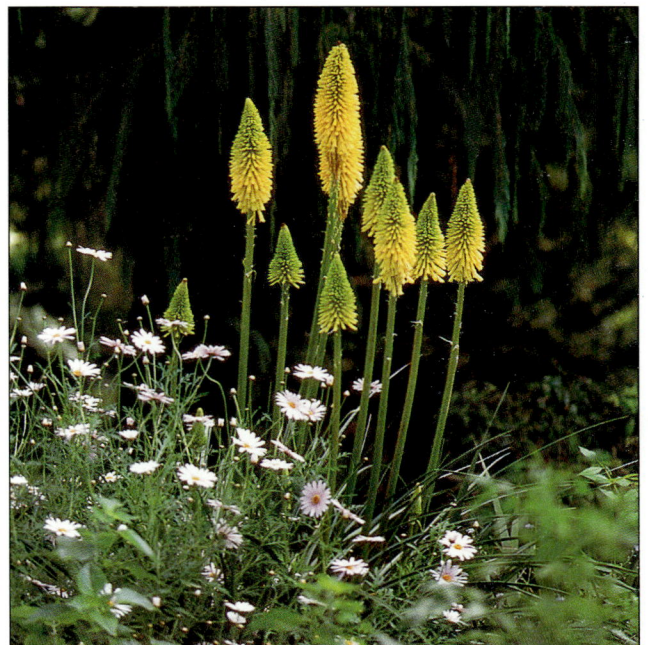

THESE GOLDEN-YELLOW, green-tipped spikes of a red hot poker cultivar provide a strong focus in this pastel border.

THE TALL, VERTICAL CLUMP of pink dahlias and the midnight blue spires of delphinium provide a colourful mix. They form a bright imaginative backdrop for the rich mix of annuals and perennials edging this beautiful garden bed, clearly illustrating the versatility of perennials.

through the winter. Plants are mailed, bare-rooted, or in small pots, having been carefully packed and labelled. On arrival, they should be planted at once. However, if the ground is frozen, or you are not ready to plant them, either unpack and water them (if necessary), and store in a bright, cool, frost-free place, or 'heel in' as a temporary measure. To do this, dig a trench large enough to contain the plant roots in a sheltered part of the garden. Finally, lay the plants on their sides, cover the roots with soil, and lightly water them.

When planting bare-rooted plants, again make sure the hole is at least twice the width of the rootball, and deep enough to take the roots without kinking them. If some roots are very long, trim them cleanly with secateurs. Hold the plant in the hole in one hand and fill the hole, poking soil between the roots. Sometimes you can make a slight mound in the centre of the hole so that the roots can be spread out over it, keeping the crown high. Make sure the crown of the plant is not buried: if necessary, lift the plant and push more soil in around the roots.

Water thoroughly immediately after planting if the soil is dry, but until the plants have developed plenty of shoot growth they will not require too much watering. The area around the plants should be mulched. If the soil has been well prepared, feeding at this time is not necessary but you may give a very light sprinkling of general fertiliser if you wish.

CARE OF PERENNIALS

Perennial plantings in areas that have been well prepared need little maintenance. You must deadhead through the flowering season to prolong blooming, and cut back or tidy up after flowering. Established perennials will only need watering in prolonged dry spells, and feeding in spring as growth commences. When they become too crowded they are divided between autumn and late winter, or early spring. This may be only necessary every three or four years. For details, see plant entries in the A-Z section.

Watering

Never give perennials a light watering because it will encourage surface rooting at the expense of a deep, root system. The plants need big, strong roots to sustain several years of growth, and benefit most from being given a deep, regular watering. On sandy soils choose such perennials as sedum, oenothera and dianthus that tolerate dry conditions. A deep mulch around the plants will help conserve moisture, as will adding quantities of organic matter to the soil as the mulch breaks down.

Feeding

Perennials should not need a lot of feeding. Apply an all-purpose plant food as growth begins; if the soil has been well prepared this should be enough for the whole growing season. If your soil is very poor though, you may like to use a slow-release granular fertiliser to feed plants through the growing season, or to apply a second helping of plant food as the flower buds start to appear. A mulch of decayed manure or compost around the plants serves two functions. It improves the soil condition, and also supplies small amounts of nutrients to the plants.

Keep the entire area free of weeds until the plants cover the ground. This will ensure that any fertiliser you apply will feed your perennials and not any unwanted weeds. Avoid high nitrogen fertilisers as they tend to promote leaf growth at the expense of flowers. Rose food is ideal.

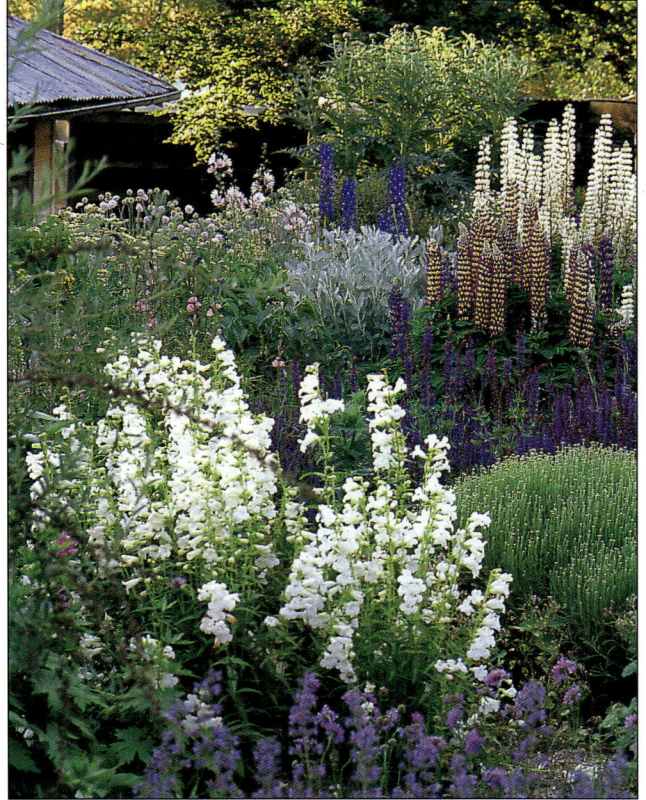

THE PENSTEMONS AND SALVIAS in the foreground make a gorgeous foil for the stiff, upright growth of Russell lupins.

Cutting flowers and deadheading

A number of perennials make very good cut flowers, and many are grown for the cut flower trade. The various daisies, chrysanthemums, Russell lupins, delphiniums, pinks and Peruvian lilies are just a few of the perennials that are commercially grown. Regularly picking the flowers will help to ensure a long succession of bloom. If the flowers are not removed they will mature, most setting seed so that the flowering cycle will finish abruptly as the plant decides its reproductive work is over. If you do not want to take cut flowers, remember to deadhead regularly.

Exceptions to this rule are plants such as cardoon and globe thistle that have decorative seedheads. Some gardeners prefer to leave them on the plant. Many remain attractive even when dry, and they can add interest to the garden in late autumn and winter, especially when covered in frost or snow.

AFTER FLOWERING

After the flowering season is over, perennials can be cut back almost to the ground. If you live in an area prone to heavy frosts, some of the more tender perennials will then need to have the crown of the plant covered. A thick layer of straw, or autumn leaves, held in place by a few sticks in windy sites, will protect them from winter damage.

Alternatively, you could leave some stems sticking out of the ground to create extra, interesting shapes over winter. Grasses are especially invaluable. They are at their best when covered with frost or snow, or when helping to cast a web of shadows from the low winter sun. The birds also benefit from the seedheads.

THE BRIGHT, HOT COLOURS of orange and yellow feature in this very effective planting, which shows up so impressively against the cool green of the lawn. The large clump of red hot pokers and a generous drift of deep apricot-orange geum are especially notable.

INCREASING YOUR STOCK OF PERENNIALS

Division

Clumps of perennials are divided either when they become congested, or when you want to plant sections elsewhere in the garden. In general, most perennials need dividing about every three or four years, possibly longer. Division is done after flowering or while the plants are dormant.

If you want some pieces to plant elsewhere you can sever a section with a knife, or put a spade through the clump, and lift away what you want. This might lose some of the peripheral pieces but the process is quick and simple. Otherwise, dig up the whole clump, shake off the excess soil and pull the clump apart or cut it into sections. Replant the sections immediately, trimming off very long roots. Remember that the outer growths are the youngest, to be saved, and that the centre of the plant may have died, in which case it can be discarded. You may need to divide very large, heavy clumps by pushing two garden forks, back to back, into the centre to prise it apart. A sharp spade may also be used but this needs a lot of force and will, of course, result in the loss of some sections of plant. This may not be of any consequence with vigorous perennials.

If you are unable to replant at once or have pieces to give away, wrap them in damp newspaper or hessian and keep in a shaded, sheltered spot, giving time to decide where to plant them. 'Heeling in', as described on the previous page, is another way to store plants temporarily, and they are less likely to dry out. They can, of course, be potted up in a good quality potting mix.

Taking cuttings

Many perennial plants can be grown from cuttings and a number, including geraniums and diascias, are among the easiest plants to strike. Others that will grow readily from cuttings include penstemons and sedums.

Make a mix of two or three parts of coarse sand and one of peat, or peat substitute compost. Put the prepared mix in clean pots, preferably no larger than 10cm (4in) across. A pot of this size will take a good number of cuttings which will not be forced to sit in a large amount of soil that remains wet when watered, taking too long to dry out, consequently rotting the roots.

Take tip cuttings of unflowered shoots, no more than 5–10cm (2–4in) long. Cut, do not tear, pieces from the parent plant. Take the cuttings early in the morning, placing the pieces in a clean plastic bag, and quickly put in a cool, shady place. Trim the cuttings by removing the lower leaves, allowing just a very few to remain on top. Cleanly cut the base of the cutting below a node (leaf junction). Another aid to rooting is to 'wound' the cutting by carefully scraping about 1cm (3/8in) of the outer bark or stem cover at the base of the stem. Hormone rooting powders can also be used but are not usually necessary with most perennials.

Use a clean stick or pencil to make a hole in the compost. Put the cutting in the hole and carefully firm the surrounding mix. Once all your cuttings are in the pot you can water them thoroughly and put the pot in a warm, sheltered place out of direct sun. In warm months geraniums and daisies may be well rooted after three weeks, but many plants can take a considerable time. Check regularly to see if the cuttings need water but do not keep them wet or, as explained they will rot.

DIVIDING A CLUMP

Step 1: Use a garden fork to lift the whole perennial clump from the soil.

Step 2: Separate matted clumps by inserting two garden forks, back to back, firmly into the clump.

Step 3: First press the fork handles together, and then force them apart to split the clump in two. Repeat until the clumps are the size you want.

Step 4: Use secateurs to cut off dead, rotten or damaged roots. The clumps are now ready for replanting.

STRIKING A CUTTING

Step 1: Take a cutting just below a leaf node or joint. Use a sharp knife or secateurs so that the cutting is not bruised. Trim it if necessary.

Step 2: Make a hole in the compost with your finger and insert the cutting into it. Firm the soil gently around it. If you are placing more than one cutting in the pot, plant them around the edge, giving them plenty of space.

Step 3: Water the cuttings in well, but take care not to dislodge them. Make sure the water is draining away well as the cuttings will rot if the soil remains wet.

Step 4: To make a humid atmosphere and keep the soil and cuttings moist, make a frame of sticks or wire tall enough to cover the cuttings. Place a polythene bag over the frame, and stand the pot out of direct sunlight.

A ROMANTIC GARDEN PATH is bordered by old-fashioned favourites, including perennial daisies and scented pinks.

Taking root cuttings

A number of plants, including perennials such as sea lavender, romneya and perennial phlox, can be grown from root cuttings. As the plant will be disturbed when the cuttings are taken, this task is best done in winter.

• Remove the soil from around the base of the plant until you reach the roots. Trace them back until they are 3–5mm ($\frac{1}{8}$–$\frac{3}{16}$in) thick, and cut off some cleanly with a sharp knife or secateurs. Immediately place them in a plastic bag so they do not dry out.

• Wash the soil from the roots and cut them into 2.5–5cm (1–2in) lengths. If you intend to plant them vertically you will need to know which way is up; cut all the tops straight across and the bottoms at an angle.

• Place the cuttings vertically in a container, or lay them in horizontally and cover with about 5mm ($\frac{3}{16}$in) of John Innes No.1. Water thoroughly and check regularly to see whether further watering is needed.

• Once good shoots have appeared, your new plants can be potted up individually into small pots or planted into the ground. It is important to keep the cuttings moist, but if you saturate the compost the roots will rot.

WHAT CAN GO WRONG?

Perennials can be attacked by a number of insect pests and diseases, and problems that occur on specific plants will be discussed in the individual plant entries. Slugs and snails are among the worst pests for herbaceous perennials since they can destroy newly emerging growth as it appears in spring. If each successive burst of leaves is destroyed, the plant will eventually give up. You must search for and destroy these pests, perhaps picking them off by hand, or using bait or beer traps.

Overwatering or poorly drained heavy soils can also damage or kill perennials, especially if they are too wet during their dormant period when there is no foliage to transpire moisture from the plant. Waterlogged soils also provide ideal conditions for the growth and spread of various soil-borne, root-rotting fungi. A few plants, such as astilbe and hosta, actually enjoy damp or boggy ground, but most enjoy conditions with good drainage.

Yellow leaves
• Plants may have been overwatered or they may be too dry. You are actually more likely to overwater a perennial in a pot than in a border. They may also need feeding if this has not been done for some time. Try a light application of fertiliser; in warm weather there should be an improvement within two to three weeks. Towards the end of the growing season you can expect to see some leaf yellowing as they finish their useful life. Do not worry if a few leaves, especially down towards the ground, become brown or yellow during the active spring period.

Curled or distorted leaves
• Keep a regular check against aphids. They can be a terrible problem. They are small, sap-sucking insects that may be black, brown, green or clear. They cluster thickly on the new growth of plants, sucking out the sap. This may cause curling or distortion of leaves, and flowers may fail to open if the sap has been sucked from the buds or they, too,

A HEALTHY display of violets.

may be distorted. Close inspection usually reveals these tiny insects; they can be squashed and wiped off the stems, hosed off or sprayed with insecticidal soap or pyrethrum-based sprays. Aphids need to be controlled as they also transmit virus diseases from plant to plant.

Silvery mottling on foliage
• Silver markings or discolouration of foliage may be the first sign of thrip attack. These tiny insects attack plant tissue and suck the sap. Unlike most sap-sucking insects they attack the top, not the under leaf. There are several different types that cause plant damage. They are readily recognisable, usually having black bodies and wings edged with hairs. Apart from the physical damage, some thrips are also responsible for transmitting virus diseases from plant to plant. Since many thrips use weeds as hosts it is important to keep them out of your beds and borders. If thrips are causing damage, make sure that the plants are not stressed through lack of water. When spraying, use an appropriate contact or systemic insecticide.

Curled and browned flowers
• Check plants for thrips because they can attack pale-coloured flowers. For their control, see 'Silvery mottling on foliage'.

TAKING ROOT CUTTINGS

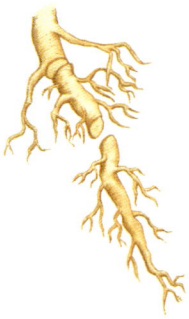

Step 1: To take root cuttings from most perennials, trace the roots back and cut out a section some 3–5mm ($\frac{1}{8}$–$\frac{3}{16}$in) thick.

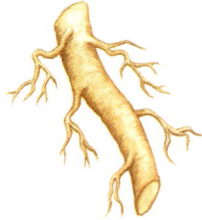

Step 2: Wash any soil from the roots and cut them into sections 2.5–5cm (1-2in) long. Mark the top of each so you know which way up to plant them.

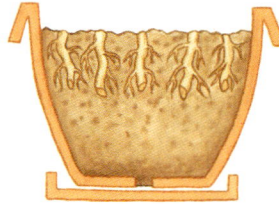

Step 3: Place the root cuttings vertically in a container, making sure that they are the right way up. Water them in thoroughly.

Alternatively, if plants have thin roots, take cuttings in the same way but lay them horizontally and cover with a thin layer of compost.

Holes in leaves or on leaf edges
• If your plants have chewed edges or large areas of leaf missing, check for snails. They are the most likely culprits. Pick the snails off and destroy them, or use a bait if you do not have a pet.
• If there is no sign of snails, start looking for caterpillars. Chewing insects such as caterpillars can do a great deal of damage in quite a short time because they can be such voracious feeders. They can be well camouflaged, lying along leaf margins or hiding under leaves. Try first to find and destroy them, but if the damage continues, dust the plants with derris.

Mottled leaves
• Leaf mottling may be the result of mite damage. Mites are not true insects, having eight legs like other members of the arachnid family. Mites are sap suckers, and foliage attacked by mites appears mottled and discoloured. With the aid of a magnifying glass the tiny creatures and their clear circular eggs can sometimes be seen on the underside of leaves. If severe mite attacks go unnoticed initially, there may be fine webbing on the underside of foliage too. Sometimes with light attacks hosing under the leaves every two to three days is enough to reduce their population to an acceptable, non-

damaging level. Mites are much worse in warm, dry weather or on plants that may be sheltered by the overhanging eaves of a house. Make sure that plants are well watered and well nourished. If mite numbers do reach unacceptable levels, clearly getting out of hand, you may need to spray with an appropriate insecticide. Many general, broad spectrum insecticides are useless against mites.

Grey/white powder on leaves
• This is probably caused by the common fungal disease, powdery mildew. In humid areas this disease is a constant problem. For plants that are very susceptible to powdery mildew, much work is being done to breed plant-resistant varieties. Meanwhile, it may be necessary to spray with a fungicide such as carbendazim or copper oxychloride or, alternatively, you can dust the plants with sulphur. If you have any

A VIBRANT show of argyranthemums.

kind of problem with powdery mildew, avoid watering the plants late in the day so that you do not increase the humidity around them overnight.

Black or dark spots on leaves
• There are many strains of fungal leaf spots that can attack a wide range of plants. If only a few leaves are affected, remove and destroy them. Avoid watering late in the day and, where possible, avoid splashing the foliage which will spread the fungal spores. Many fungal leaf spots respond well to simple fungicides such as copper oxychloride, but there are other effective fungicides available to the home gardener.

Yellow spots on top of leaves
• Yellow spots on the upper side of leaves that have blisters, or pustules on the underside, are likely to be some form of rust. There is an enormous number of rust strains, and they can attack a wide range of plants and perennials, including chrysanthemums. It is a good idea to remove the worst affected leaves immediately, and to avoid overhead watering which quickly splashes the spores around, increasing contamination. Copper oxychloride will control some rusts, though you may find you need to use a more specific fungicide.

PLANNING A PERENNIAL GARDEN

Many perennials have a long flowering period, and well-planned beds of perennials can display a succession of flowers over many months. This does, however, take a good deal of planning and probably some trial and error.

If you are planting a large area, it's best to design it on paper first so that you can place the tallest plants at the back or in the centre of the bed, also giving you time to devise your colour scheme. You can experiment by using a variety of plants, all with flowers in one colour or shades of one colour, or you may opt for a planting of bright contrasts. Whatever scheme you choose, allow for plenty of plants to create a full, rich scene. A well-planted perennial border or garden is close planted so that every bit of soil is covered, providing foliage and floral interest throughout the season.

ABOVE: These rich purple spikes belong to the spectacular Salvia 'Ostfriesland', a cultivar of Salvia nemorosa.

LEFT: True perennials such as purple Liatris spicata, and the yellow daisies of Coreopsis verticillata, mix well with annual red strawflowers and Dahlia 'Bishop of Llandaff'.

THE LUSH GREEN SCENE, composed of hostas, candelabra primulas, and other shade-tolerant perennials, in a fern-filled woodland garden on the mild west coast of Scotland. Such a scene can easily be reduced and modified for the borders in a shady city garden.

USING PERENNIALS

Perennials are among the most versatile of plants, and the vast majority of gardeners use them in conjunction with permanent plantings of shrubs, annuals and bulbs. They are plants that require far less work and maintenance than annuals while still giving a great deal of seasonal colour and interest. In fact many low-growing perennials, such as penstemon, lamb's ears, pinks and bergenia, make excellent border plantings, while taller growers, such as phlox and *Acanthus mollis*, can be planted among shrubs. Long-flowering plants, such as achillea and corydalis, can be used to give colour between seasonal annual displays. They also give interest to a garden bed where bulbs have finished flowering, and are in the process of dying down.

PERENNIAL BORDERS

Traditionally, perennials have often been close planted in a border. To get an idea of how a well-grown perennial border should look, visit the great gardens like Sissinghurst in Kent, and Arley Hall in Cheshire. Gardeners have been refining the art of perennial borders for a very long time, and both first-time and experienced gardeners will find plenty of new, imaginative ideas in these schemes. Specialist nurseries often have special exhibit beds where you can also see how well various perennials combine.

FORMAL GARDENS

It is difficult for a perennial garden to look really formal, but many of the best perennial schemes have been informally planted within a formal framework. Some are enclosed within walls, while many are contained within low, formally trimmed hedges. The garden beds are laid out in strict geometric style, resembling an ornate piece of embroidery when viewed from above, their angular shapes defined by tightly pruned hedges, often of box or lavender. Sometimes the garden beds are also defined by close-mown paths of grass.

Probably the closest one can get to a formal perennial scheme is by creating a mirror-planting effect. Each part of the design mirrors the next, and the sections are divided by paths of grass, brick, gravel or stone. For a mirror planting to be successful, the whole of the area must be in full sun, otherwise there is absolutely no chance of growth rates and flowering times being the same, or as near as one can get to that given you are dealing with living plant material.

PLANT ARRANGEMENT

Perennials come in many shapes and sizes, which is a great advantage when planning a garden. If your perennial garden is to be sited against a fence or wall you might decide to place the tallest growers at the back. This both forms a backbone and gives you the space to stand back and fully appreciate them. So, for example, the long tall spears of delphiniums generally stand behind their lower-growing neighbours. If you are designing an island bed, the tall plants are traditionally placed right in the centre for a formal effect, or slightly off-centre so it does not look quite so inflexibly schematic. Smaller plants radiate out, down towards the front of the border, giving a graduated, tiered effect. But such arrangements are not strictly necessary. You might prefer, instead, to give a more informal look by gently mixing heights, creating undulations. When doing this the most important point to remember is that no plant should be hidden by its neighbour, or cast in total shade, and that all should be visible from some vantage point so that you can appreciate their colour and shape.

A number of plants, such as mulleins and red hot pokers, give very strong vertical accents which contrast well with lower, more variably shaped plants. And striking foliage plants, such as cardoon and *Melianthus major*, are grown more for their strong structural shape than for their flowers. (Note that the latter is rather tender for the first two years, but once it has a shrubby base can be left outside all-year round in milder areas, provided it is given some frost protection.) These big plants must be sited carefully and probably not used to excess. A contrast in leaf colour, shape and texture will also add considerable interest to the perennial garden. If you have the luxury of being able to create a very large or long perennial border, you will need to think about repeating some of the shapes and colours to tie the planting together. The other great advantage of growing perennials is that you can move them around when they are dormant, or semi-dormant, if you are not totally satisfied with their appearance or performance. They let you modify the design.

Everyone would love to have a garden that was in full flower for months at a time. Planning to ensure a succession of blooms over many months is the hard part of designing a garden. Even if you consult the best reference books by the best writers, reliable local nurseries and experienced friends, you will find that plants behave differently in different situations; in the end what counts is personal experience. Prior research is essential, providing vital guidance, and it is worth walking around your neighbourhood to see exactly which plants are being grown successfully.

USING COLOUR

Colour is, of course, a most important consideration. If you are making a large perennial garden it is a good idea to put your planting suggestions on paper, even using coloured pencils or paints to help you see how the colours work together. You do not need to be an artist as rough shapes or blobs of colour will do. You would not want or expect to have all the plants in flower at the one time, but you need to think about overlapping flowering times.

If you want a cool looking garden you could restrict yourself to white, blue, cream or pale pink flowers, with some silver foliage plants as accents. Red, yellow and orange flowering plants will give you a hot and vibrant look. Sometimes the addition of an area of very strong colour lifts the garden out of the ordinary. Some very famous long perennial borders cover a wide colour range, starting with very soft pastel colours, ending with strong, hot colours. Another idea is to position clumps of the same plant at intervals along a border as the repetition adds to the effect of the design. Even if you have only a small space to work with, you will find the repetition gives more form to the garden.

BLUE LUPINS and white poppies provide a cool contrast with the bright reds and yellows in the extensive borders behind.

PERENNIALS FOR ALL SEASONS

At every season of the year there is some perennial plant in flower. Winter brings the delicate and subtle beauty of the winter or Lenten rose (*Helleborus* spp.), and also bergenia in mild areas. Spring brings a succession of flowers in both mild and cold districts. Columbines, armeria, Solomon's seal, candelabra primula, geum, pinks and heuchera are just a few of the lovely spring-flowering perennials. Summer brings bergamot, achillea, platycodon, and rudbeckias, some of which flower well into autumn. Autumn perennials include chrysanthemums, favoured for their garden display and cut flowers, while red hot pokers, sedum and asters provide colour and interest at a time when annuals are either being pulled out or planted for the next season. These autumn-flowering perennials, along with some autumn-flowering bulbs such as colchicums and nerines, will carry your garden beautifully into winter.

Perennials also generally combine well with spring bulbs. While the perennials are still dormant, or are just beginning to put on new growth, the bulbs flower providing a combination of foliage and blooms. Then, when the bulbs have finished performing and the foliage is beginning to look tatty and start dying, the perennials begin to take over, becoming the dominant garden feature.

ACANTHUS MOLLIS

Bear's breeches

LITTLE FLOWERS in purple and white, open along tall spikes above the foliage.

THE BEAR'S BREECHES in this Scottish garden are thriving in the open. The masses of handsome foliage suit a large garden where you can stand back and see the plants in perspective.

FEATURES

HERBACEOUS

Also known as bear's breeches, this handsome foliage plant grows from 70cm–1m (28-39in) high, and can make a clump close to 1m (39in) wide. The dark glossy leaves provided the inspiration and model for the decoration on Corinthian columns. This striking feature plant is at its best when mass planted, though one generous clump can be extremely effective in quite a small area. It enjoys full sun, but also tolerates shade. The stiff flower spikes of purple and white flowers appear among the foliage from spring into summer. It can be quite a vigorous grower although it dies back after flowering. It can multiply quickly once established, but is rarely troublesome.

ACANTHUS AT A GLANCE

A. mollis is a vigorous Mediterranean perennial liking dry, stoney ground. Hardy to −15°C (5°F), with bold shapely foliage.

JAN	/	
FEB	sow	
MAR	divide	
APR	transplant	
MAY	flowering	
JUN	flowering	
JULY	/	
AUG	/	
SEPT	/	
OCT	divide	
NOV	/	
DEC	/	

RECOMMENDED VARIETIES

Acanthus mollis 'Fielding Gold'

A.m. 'Hollard's Gold'

A.m. Latifolius Group

COMPANION PLANTS

Bergenia x 'Ballawley'

Forsythia

Gypsophila

Syringa vulgaris

CONDITIONS

Aspect It flowers best in full sun, but also grows in light shade.

Site Needs well-drained soil that contains plenty of organic matter to aid water retention. Give plants a deep layer of mulch with compost in the spring, and then a second application if necessary in mid-summer.

GROWING METHOD

Propagation Grows from seed sown in spring, or divide clumps in the spring or autumn. Plant new divisions 30–40cm (12–16in) apart. Young plants must be given ample water in dry weather during spring and summer. After flowering cut back on the watering.

Feeding Apply a complete plant food as growth starts during the spring.

Problems Since slugs and snails can cause a lot of damage to young growth, badly disfiguring it, take precautions. No other problems are known.

FLOWERING

Season The tall spikes of purple and white flowers appear in late spring and summer.

Cutting It is possible to use this as a cut flower; the dried spikes make good indoor decoration.

AFTER FLOWERING

Requirements Protect young plants with straw overwinter. Cut off the flowering stems once faded.

ACHILLEA
Yarrow

LONG-FLOWERING and not as invasive as the species, the new hybrid achilleas will give great pleasure for months.

ACHILLEA IS ALSO KNOWN as soldier's woundwort, nosebleed and sanguinary, which reflects its value in herbal medicine.

FEATURES

HERBACEOUS

Yarrow are vigorous perennials offering heights from 5cm–1.2m (2in–4ft). The species has flattish heads of white flowers and feathery foliage, but cultivars have flowers in a lovely range of shades, including yellow, pink, apricot and crimson. Flowers are long lasting. Yarrow is quick and easy to establish, and may need to be controlled, however the runners are quite easy to pull out. Some of the cultivars are less invasive than the species.
A. filipendulina has flat heads of bright yellow flowers lasting all summer. Selected forms have deep or pale yellow blooms. Best planted in large drifts, yarrow is ideal for the back of borders or among annuals.

ACHILLEA AT A GLANCE

Mainly deciduous perennials grown for their attractive, daisy-like summer and autumn flowers. Hardy to −15°C (5°F).

		RECOMMENDED VARIETIES
JAN	/	*Achillea* 'Coronation Gold'
FEB	sow	*Achillea filipendulina*
MAR	sow	'Cloth of Gold'
APR	transplant	*A. f.* 'Gold Plate'
MAY	divide	*A.* x *lewisii* "King Edward'
JUN	flowering	*A. millefolium*
JULY	flowering	'Cerise Queen'
AUG	flowering	*A. m.* 'Lilac Beauty'
SEPT	flowering	*A. m.* 'White Queen'
OCT	/	*A.* 'Moonshine'
NOV	/	*A. tomentosa*
DEC	/	

CONDITIONS

Aspect   Needs full sun for the best results, but will tolerate some shade for part of the day.
Site   Any well-drained soil is suitable.

GROWING METHOD

Propagation   Grows easily if established clumps are lifted and divided in the spring. Plant the vigorous new divisions 20–30cm (8–12in) apart, and discard the old. New, young plants need regular watering in prolonged, dry spells, but once established achillea is remarkably drought tolerant, and needs only an occasional deep drink.
Feeding   Apply a complete plant food as growth commences in spring.
Problems   No specific pest or disease problems are known to attack achillea.

FLOWERING

Season   The long flowering period lasts throughout summer into early autumn. Regular removal of the spent, fading flower stems will significantly prolong blooming.
Cutting   The flowers are good for cutting because they have a reasonably long vase life. Take handfuls of cut flowers for the vase as soon as the heads are fully open. Also excellent for drying.

AFTER FLOWERING

Requirements   Cut off any spent flower stalks that remain on the plant in late autumn.

AGAPANTHUS

African blue lily

THE BLUE AND WHITE flowering heads of agapanthus are composed of numerous flowers. They make a striking feature.

THIS DENSE PLANTING of agapanthus needs little attention and rewards the gardener with its wonderful summer flowers.

FEATURES

Agapanthus has dark green, strap-shaped leaves that grow to about 50cm (20in) long. It produces rounded heads of blue or white flowers on top of stems 1m (39in) or more high, but even without the flowers it makes a great foliage accent. It is hardy in the south and west, but in colder regions needs winter protection. The Headbourne hybrids are particularly hardy. It can be grown in containers, and looks excellent in eye-catching tubs. Several attractive dwarf forms have foliage that rarely exceed 20cm (8in).

CONDITIONS

Aspect   Tolerates some shade, but the flowering will be poor. Full sun is ideal.

AGAPANTHUS AT A GLANCE

A vigorous perennial, forming bold, eye-catching flowering clumps, from southern Africa. Many hardy to –5ºC (23ºF).

		RECOMMENDED VARIETIES
JAN	/	
FEB	sow	*Agapanthus africanus*
MAR	sow	*A. a.* 'Albus'
APR	divide	*A. caulescens*
MAY	transplant	'Lilliput'
JUN	/	'Loch Hope'
JULY	flowering	'Peter Pan'
AUG	flowering	*A. praecox* 'Variegatus'
SEPT	flowering	
OCT	/	
NOV	/	
DEC	/	

Site   Grows in almost any soil, but well-drained ground with organic matter is perfect. In colder gardens, grow by a south-facing wall.

GROWING METHOD

Propagation   Divide clumps in the spring, ensuring that each division has a crown and a decent batch of healthy roots. The latter can be shortened and some outer leaves removed if necessary. Plant about 25cm (10in) apart. Also grows from seed sown in the spring. Needs regular watering to establish, but once settled it can cope with long, dry periods. However, for the best growth and flowering, do not let new young plants dry out.

Feeding   Apply complete plant food in the early spring. Potted plants will perform better with an application of slow-release granules, or a monthly liquid feed, carefully following the manufacturer's recommended rate.

Problems   There are no particular problems, but clumps will harbour groups of snails. Pick off.

FLOWERING

Season   Blooms appear in mid- to late summer, depending on the conditions.

Cutting   Agapanthus can be used as a cut flower if the stems are plunged into boiling water for 15 seconds immediately after cutting.

AFTER FLOWERING

Requirements   No pruning needed other than cutting off spent flower stems and dead leaves. Protect crowns over winter with a thick mulch of straw or dry leaves.

ALCHEMILLA MOLLIS

Lady's mantle

LONG USED as a folk medicine to help heal wounds and gynaecological problems, lady's mantle is today usually grown for its decorative value, and ability to self-seed. The pure lime-green flowers brighten the garden, making a marvellous contrast against the wide, lobed leaves.

FEATURES

HERBACEOUS

This is a quick-growing herbaceous perennial mostly used as a border plant to edge paths and beds. An abundant self-seeder, it is good for suppressing weeds, filling any free spaces, often popping up in cracks in paving. Growing anywhere between 20–40cm (8–16in) high, one plant may spread to 28–40cm (11–16in). The rounded, slightly hairy leaves overlap one another, and the plant produces trusses of bright lime-green flowers through summer. It provides a lovely contrast with other, stronger colours. The leaves tend to trap raindrops or dew, adding to the effect.

ALCHEMILLA AT A GLANCE

A. mollis is a hardy perennial grown for its prolific self-seeding, and attractive lime-green foliage. Hardy to –15ºC (5ºF).

		COMPANION PLANTS
JAN	/	
FEB	sow	Delphinium
MAR	sow	Dicentra
APR	transplant	Eremurus
MAY	transplant	Eucomis
JUN	flowering	Euonymus
JULY	flowering	Geranium
AUG	flowering	Gladiolus
SEPT	flowering	Lupin
OCT	divide	Rose
NOV	/	
DEC	/	

CONDITIONS

Aspect   Thrives in full sun, though it tolerates a degree of light shade.

Site   Needs well-drained soil that has a high organic content.

GROWING METHOD

Propagation   Self-sown seedlings can be easily transplanted to other positions. Clumps can be divided in the spring or autumn with the divisions spaced 20–25cm (8–10in) apart. Newly planted specimens may need watering, but mature plants tolerate dry periods. Justifiably known as a great survivor and spreader.

Feeding   Apply a complete plant food as the new growth begins.

Problems   No specific problems are known.

FLOWERING

Season   Masses of lime-green flowers appear from late spring through summer.

Cutting   A great favourite with flower arrangements.

AFTER FLOWERING

Requirements If you do not want plants to self-seed, trim spent flowers as soon as they fade. Once flowering has finished and growth begins to die down, the plants can be cut back hard with shears, or even a trimmer if you want to be ruthless.

ALSTROEMERIA
Peruvian Lily

ALSO KNOWN AS THE LILY of the Incas, the Peruvian lily can be placed in a mixed perennial border as here, or planted between shrubs. Bold groupings are best. Gardeners can choose from a colourful range of species and cultivars, but may be unable to obtain some of the varieties sold by florists.

FEATURES

HERBACEOUS

The Peruvian lily is grown commercially on a large scale as the flowers are long lasting when cut. In the garden it is a herbaceous perennial with flower spikes growing mostly 30–60cm (12–24in) high, although there are dwarf forms and very tall ones. The flowers are beautifully marked with streaks and spots of colour, contrasting with a wide range of base colours of cream, yellow, orange, pink and red. If conditions suit, these plants spread by means of fleshy rhizomes (roots) to form large clumps. Also excellent when grown in pots.

ALSTROEMERIA AT A GLANCE

A hardy perennial surviving –10ºC (14ºF). Grown for their excellent showy flowers, many make unbeatable cut flowers.

JAN	/	
FEB	/	
MAR	/	**RECOMMENDED VARIETIES**
APR	sow	*Alstroemeria ligtu* hybrids
MAY	/	'Orange Gem'
JUN	transplant	'Orange Glory'
JULY	flowering	'Princess Mira' (and all
AUG	flowering	'Princess' varieties)
SEPT	flowering	'Solent Crest'
OCT	divide	
NOV	/	
DEC	/	

CONDITIONS

Aspect   Needs full sun and shelter to thrive, especially in colder areas. Also requires shelter from strong wind. Makes an excellent potted, greenhouse plant.

Site   Must have very free-draining soil containing plenty of decayed organic matter.

GROWING METHOD

Propagation   Many grow readily from seed sown in spring, but division of established clumps is easiest; spring is generally considered the best time. Bare-root plants can be hard to establish; pot-grown plants, available in the summer, are better. Plant roots 5cm (2in) deep and about 15cm (6in) apart. In a prolonged dry period, water bedded plants regularly in spring and summer, but restrict watering after flowering.

Feeding   Apply slow-release granular fertiliser in spring.

Problems   No specific problems are known.

FLOWERING

Season   Most species and their cultivars flower from spring into summer, some into autumn.

Cutting   This is a first-class cut flower.

AFTER FLOWERING

Requirements   Cut off spent flower stems at ground level. Protect crowns with straw in cold winters.

ANEMONE X HYBRIDA

Windflower (Anemone x hybrida, syn. A. hupehensis var. japonica)

ELEGANT SIMPLICITY is the best way to describe the form of the Japanese anemone with its white, yellow and green colour scheme.

RELIABLE IN BLOOM year after year, the Japanese anemone is an attractive garden addition, softening stiff, geometric schemes.

FEATURES

HERBACEOUS

Also known as the Japanese windflower, this herbaceous perennial is one of the great joys of the autumn garden. The leaves are three-lobed, somewhat maple-like, and the single or double flowers are carried on stems up to 1m (39in) high. Flowers may be single or double-coloured white, pale or deep pink. Once established, they spread into large clumps quite rapidly, travelling by underground stems, and also self-seeding. Some consider them invasive but plants can be easily dug out, and a mass planting in full bloom is a real delight. Grow where they can remain undisturbed for some years. Site at the back of a shady bed or in dappled sunlight under trees.

ANEMONE AT A GLANCE

A. x hybrida is a free-flowering, quick spreading herbaceous perennial with lovely, pale pink flowers. Hardy to −15°C (5°F).

JAN	/	
FEB	/	
MAR	divide	
APR	transplant	
MAY	/	
JUN	/	
JULY	/	
AUG	flowering	
SEPT	flowering	
OCT	sow	
NOV	/	
DEC	/	

RECOMMENDED VARIETIES

Anemone x hybrida
  'Honorine Jobert'
A. x h. 'Konigin Charlotte'
A. x h. 'Luise Uhink'
A. x h. 'Margarete'
A. x h. 'Pamina'
A. x h. 'Richard Ahrends'

CONDITIONS

Aspect   Prefers shade or semi-shade with shelter from strong winds.

Site   Grows best in well-drained soil that contains plenty of organic matter.

GROWING METHOD

Propagation   Increase from root cuttings in winter, or divide established clumps in early spring, ensuring that each division has a decent set of roots. This vigorous plant can sometimes be tricky to divide and transplant. Replant the new, vigorous younger growths from the outside of the clump, generally about 30cm (12in) apart. New young plants need ample watering in prolonged dry spells during the growing season.

Feeding   Fertilising is not essential, but a complete plant food can be applied in the spring.

Problems   No specific problems are known.

FLOWERING

Season   Flowers appear prolifically from late summer through the autumn months.

Cutting   Though they seem perfect for cut flower displays, the flowers do not last that well.

AFTER FLOWERING

Requirements   Cut back spent flower stems to ground level once they begin to fade, and cut the plant right back to the ground in late autumn.

AQUILEGIA
Columbine

WIDELY CONTRASTING COLOURS successfully combine in the flowers of this modern, long-spurred hybrid columbine.

AN OPEN WOODLAND SETTING is ideal for columbines, letting them freely self-seed forming, bold, distinctive groups.

FEATURES

HERBACEOUS

These old-fashioned favourites, also called granny's bonnets, give a fine display in the garden and make decorative cut flowers. The foliage is often blue-green, and the flowers come in single colours – white, pink, crimson, yellow and blue – and combinations of pastel and brighter shades. There are also excellent black and whites ('Magpie'). The older forms have short-spurred flowers that resemble old-fashioned bonnets, especially 'Nora Barlow', a good double which is a mix of red, pink and green. Modern hybrids are long spurred, and available in many single colours and bicolours. Plants may be 40–70cm (16–28in) high. Columbines are not long lived but are easily seed grown. Ideal for the dappled garden, grow them under deciduous trees and in borders.

AQUILEGIA AT A GLANCE

A clump-forming perennial, happy in semi-shade, perfect for the cottage garden where it freely self-seeds. Hardy to –15°C (5°F).

		RECOMMENDED VARIETIES
JAN	/	*Aquilegia bertolonii*
FEB	/	*A. canadensis*
MAR	sow	*A. flabellata*
APR	transplant	*A. f.* var. *pumila*
MAY	flowering	*A. f.* var. *f. alba*
JUN	flowering	'Henson Harebell'
JULY	/	'Magpie'
AUG	/	Music series
SEPT	divide	*A. vulgaris* 'Nora Barlow'
OCT	sow	
NOV	/	
DEC	/	

CONDITIONS

Aspect Prefers semi-shade, and thrives in woodland gardens, but full sun is not a problem.
Site Needs well-drained soil that contains plenty of organic matter.

GROWING METHOD

Propagation Clumps are actually quite hard to divide, but it can be done, autumn being the best time. Columbine also grows from seed sown in early spring, or in the autumn. Self-sown plants are hardy, but note that they may not always be true to type. Space plants about 30cm (12in) apart. New young plants must not be allowed to dry out in prolonged dry spells in the spring and summer months. Keep a careful watch.
Feeding Apply complete plant food in the spring as the new growth begins to emerge.
Problems No particular pest or disease problems are known for this plant.

FLOWERING

Season There is a long flowering period from mid-spring to mid-summer.
Cutting Flower stems can be cut for the vase, and they make an attractive display, but the garden show lasts considerably longer.

AFTER FLOWERING

Requirements Spent flower stems can either be removed or left on the plants enabling the seeds to mature. Cut back the old growth to ground level as it dies off.

ARMERIA MARITIMA
Sea thrift

EACH FLOWERHEAD resembles a tiny posy, which is why thrift makes a fine cut flower, alone or in a composition with other flowers.

POOR STONY GROUND, which resembles thrift's natural habitat, provides ideal conditions for growing this plant.

FEATURES

EVERGREEN

Also known as sea thrift, this evergreen perennial grows in little grassy mounds 5–12.5cm (2–5in) high. It occurs naturally in northern Europe and around the Mediterranean, often in very exposed situations, including cliff tops. The rounded flowerheads are carried above the foliage on stems 15–30cm (6–12in) high. Flowers vary in colour in the species and may be white, pink or almost red, and there are a number of named cultivars available. Thrift can be used as a groundcover or edging plant, or can be planted in rockeries, on dry walls, or in poor soil where few other plants will survive. It also makes a good container plant.

ARMERIA AT A GLANCE

A. maritima is an attractive evergreen, clump-forming perennial which colonises inhospitable areas. Hardy to –18°C (0°F).

		RECOMMENDED VARIETIES
JAN	/	
FEB	/	*Armeria maritima* 'Alba'
MAR	division	*A. m.* 'Corsica'
APR	/	*A. m.* 'Launcheana'
MAY	transplant	*A. m.* 'Ruby Glow'
JUN	flowering	*A. m.* 'Splendens'
JULY	flowering	*A. m.* 'Vindictive'
AUG	flowering	
SEPT	/	
OCT	/	
NOV	/	
DEC	/	

CONDITIONS

Aspect Needs full sun all day. Thrift tolerates dry, windy conditions and salt spray, and is an excellent choice for coastal gardens.

Site Grows in any kind of soil so long as it is very well drained. Adding sharp sand will improve the drainage.

GROWING METHOD

Propagation Divide established clumps in the spring and replant about 15–20cm (6–8in) apart. The species can be grown from seed sown in the spring, or from semi-ripe cuttings taken in the summer

Feeding Give a light dressing of complete fertiliser in early spring.

Problems Thrift has a tendency to rot if soils are in any way too heavy, poorly drained or overwatered. In humid weather and in sheltered positions it may also be susceptible to the fungal disease which is called rust. Use a fungicide to attack the problem.

FLOWERING

Season Thrift has a long flowering period through spring and summer, provided the plants are deadheaded regularly.

Cutting Makes a good cut flower.

AFTER FLOWERING

Requirements Regularly remove spent flower stems to give a prolonged flowering period.

ASTER
Michaelmas daisy

RICH MAUVE *flowers virtually obscuring the foliage on a mature plant.*

THE ATTRACTIVE Aster ericoides, *which has produced many excellent cultivars.*

ONE OF *the best of the reds is the low growing 'Winston Churchill'.*

FEATURES

HERBACEOUS

There is a wide variety of asters, and all of them flower in late summer and autumn. The most commonly grown is *A. novi-belgii*, which has a range of cultivars from dwarf forms 25cm (10in) high to tall varieties reaching 1m (39in). Flowers are blue, violet, pink, red or white, and all are good for cutting. *A. ericoides* has very small leaves and produces stems of white flowers up to 1m (39in) high. *A. x frikartii* grows about 76cm (30in) high and has violet-blue flowers. These plants are all extremely easy to grow and tolerate a wide range of conditions. They multiply readily. Taller varieties need staking.

ASTER AT A GLANCE

Hardy perennials creating large clumps, giving strong autumn colour in most situations. Hardy to –15°C (5°F).

Jan	/	
Feb	sow	
Mar	sow	
Apr	divide	
May	transplant	
Jun	/	
July	flowering	
Aug	flowering	
Sept	flowering	
Oct	divide	
Nov	/	
Dec	/	

RECOMMENDED VARIETIES

Aster alpinus
A. amellus 'Framfieldii'
A. a. 'Jacqueline Genebrier'
'Coombe Fishacre'
A. ericoides 'Golden Spray'
A. x frikartii 'Monch'
A. novae-angliae
A. novi-belgii 'Audrey'

CONDITIONS

Aspect Grows best in full sun. Tolerates light shade, but blooming may not be so prolific and growth will be less compact.

Site Add well-rotted organic matter to the soil. Feed and water well to counter disease.

GROWING METHOD

Propagation Divide clumps in late winter. These plants are prolific growers and one plant will multiply itself tenfold in a season. Replant divisions 20cm (8in) apart. The best results are from regular watering during the spring and summer, especially in long, dry periods.

Feeding Apply complete plant food in early spring.

Problems Powdery mildew can be a major problem, especially with varieties of *A. novi-belgii*. Mildew resistant varieties include *A. x frikartii* and varieties of *A. amellus*.

FLOWERING

Season The long flowering display lasts from late summer into autumn.

Cutting Cut flowers last very well if given a frequent change of water.

AFTER FLOWERING

Requirements Cut off spent flower stems close to ground level after blooming. Plants will gradually die back, but should not need more close attention until new growth appears next spring.

ASTILBE HYBRIDS
Astilbe

SOFT AND FEATHERY, *the pale pink plumes on this astilbe will provide a long display of bright flowers and fern-like foliage.*

UPRIGHT SIDE BRANCHES *are an unusual feature of this deep pink astilbe cultivar. They give an eye-catching, stiff appearance.*

FEATURES

HERBACEOUS

These perennial hybrids revel in moist soil and light shade, although they can be grown in an open, sunny position if well watered. The shiny, compound leaves are quite attractive, with astilbe also bearing tall plumes of soft flowers 50cm (20in) or more high, in shades of pink, red, mauve or white. They look best when mass planted, and are ideal for surrounding ponds, or naturalising in a wild garden. They can be used as cut flowers, but they are probably best left in the garden where their big, theatrical effect can be enjoyed for much longer. They can quickly flag in a heat wave; water at the first sign of wilting.

ASTILBE AT A GLANCE

A rhizomatous perennial that enjoys damp soil. Striking, tall flowerheads can reach 1.2m (4ft) high. Hardy to −15°C (5°F).

		RECOMMENDED VARIETIES
JAN	/	
FEB	sow	*Astilbe* x *arendsii*
MAR	divide	'Brautschleier'
APR	transplant	A. x *a.* 'Bronce Elegans'
MAY	flowering	A. x *a.* 'Fanal'
JUN	flowering	A. x *a.* 'Irrlicht'
JULY	flowering	A. x *a* 'Snowdrift'
AUG	flowering	A. x *crispa* 'Perkeo'
SEPT	flowering	'Rheinland'
OCT	/	A. *simplicifolia*
NOV	divide	'Sprite'
DEC	/	

CONDITIONS

Aspect These are versatile plants, performing equally well in bright sun and dappled shade.

Site The ideal soil is rich in organic matter and retains plenty of moisture. Regular, heavy applications of mulch are essential.

GROWING METHOD

Propagation Divide clumps in late autumn, ensuring that each division has a crown and a decent set of roots. Plant at 20–25cm (8–10in) spacings. New young plants need plenty of water in prolonged dry spells in the spring and summer months. Do not let them dry out.

Feeding Apply a general fertiliser as growth starts in the spring, and repeat 6–8 weeks later.

Problems No specific problems are known.

FLOWERING

Season Flowers from late spring through the summer. The flower display is longer lasting in a cooler summer.

Cutting Flowers can be cut for indoor decoration.

AFTER FLOWERING

Requirements Spent flowerheads will turn a pleasant rich brown colour, and are quite attractive through the winter months. They add considerable interest to the garden. Do not cut back spent flower stems to ground level until the following spring.

ASTRANTIA MAJOR
Masterwort

ASTRANTIA MAJOR *'HADSPEN BLOOD' is a striking, vibrant red, more of an eye-catcher than the species which is much whiter. Both can be used to link and soften more permanent shrubby features, or as part of a free-flowing, flowery display for late spring and early summer.*

FEATURES

HERBACEOUS

Also known as masterwort, *Astrantia major* is a 'must' for the cottage garden. A clump-forming perennial producing delightful sprays of green or pink, sometimes reddish flowers, surrounded by green-veined white bracts. A native of central Europe, it grows about 60cm (24in) high, forming clumps 45cm (18in) wide. Flowering in early and mid-summer, it can be left to colonise areas of dappled shade, though it also enjoys full sun. There are some excellent cultivars including the new 'Hadspen Blood', a striking blood red, 'Shaggy' with long bracts, and 'Sunningdale Variegated' with pale pink bracts and yellow/cream leaves. Best in large clumps.

ASTRANTIA AT A GLANCE

A. major is a clump-forming perennial grown for its abundant, attractive flowers. Excellent cultivars. Hardy to −18°C (0°F).

		RECOMMENDED VARIETIES
JAN	/	*Astrantia major alba*
FEB	/	*A. m.* 'Claret'
MAR	divide	*A. m.* 'Hadspen Blood'
APR	divide	*A. m. involucrata* 'Shaggy'
MAY	transplant	*A. m. rosea*
JUN	flowering	*A. m. rubra*
JULY	flowering	*A. m.* 'Sunningdale
AUG	sowing	Variegated'
SEPT	/	
OCT	/	
NOV	/	
DEC	/	

CONDITIONS

Aspect Thrives in either dappled shade, or in a more open sunny position.

Soil Likes compost-rich, moist, fertile soil, though it will also tolerate drier conditions. Woodland gardens and streamsides are ideal.

GROWING METHOD

Propagation Can either be grown from seed sown in late summer, once ripe, or by spring division. Plant out at least 45cm (18in) apart, or closer for an immediate covering. Do not let young plants begin to dry out in a prolonged dry spring or summer spell. The variants do not require such moist conditions, and will tolerate drier soil.

Feeding Lay a mulch around the plants in spring. This has two advantages – it enriches the soil and also prevents moisture loss.

Problems Slugs can be a major problem, attacking the stems and foliage. Pick off when seen. Powdery mildew can also strike; spray against attacks.

FLOWERING

Season The one flowering spell is in early and mid-summer.

Cutting Makes good cut flowers, which can be used to soften a stiff, structural arrangement, or as part of a more flowery display.

AFTER FLOWERING

Requirements Cut down the spent flower stems, and tidy up the foliage.

AURINIA SAXATILIS

Golden dust

A SHARP, ATTRACTIVE CONTRAST with the bright yellow flowers of golden dust, against clusters of green, spoon-shape foliage.

YELLOW AND BLUE always make a lively colour combination, as this wonderful planting of golden dust and Italian lavender proves.

FEATURES

SUMMER AUTUMN WINTER SPRING

EVERGREEN

This is a little, rounded, evergreen perennial that can grow from 10–30cm (4–12in) high, forming a mound up to 40–50cm (16–20in) across. In the species the flowers are a clear yellow, but the various cultivars produce flowers in white, cream, lemon or rich gold. Since its natural habitat is rocky, mountainous country it is ideal for a rock garden, for dry, sloping ground, or for edging garden beds provided the drainage is excellent. It is also ideally suited to troughs and the edges of large pots perhaps containing a shrub. Although golden dust is a perennial, some gardeners grow it as part of an annual spring display.

AURINIA AT A GLANCE

A. saxatilis is an evergreen, hardy perennial forming decent clumps topped by yellow flowers. Hardy to −18°C (0°F).

JAN	/	
FEB	/	**RECOMMENDED VARIETIES**
MAR	transplant	*Aurinia saxatilis* 'Citrina'
APR	/	*A. s.* 'Compacta'
MAY	flowering	*A. s.* 'Dudley Nevill'
JUN	flowering	*A. s.* 'Goldkugel'
JULY	/	*A. s.* 'Silver Queen'
AUG	/	
SEPT	/	**COMPANION PLANTS**
OCT	sow	*Aurinia corymbosa*
NOV	/	Aubrieta
DEC	/	

CONDITIONS

Aspect   Needs an open position in full sun.
Site   Soil must contain plenty of chalk, sand or grit, and be free draining but not rich.

GROWING METHOD

Propagation   Grows readily from seed sown in the autumn. Cultivars can be grown from tip cuttings taken in late spring and early summer. Space the plants about 10cm (4in) apart, giving them plenty of growing room. Aurinia is sold among the alpines at garden centres.

Feeding   Small amounts only of complete plant food may be given in early spring as a boost, but feeding is not essential.

Problems   No specific problems are known besides poor drainage. Overwatering pot-grown specimens can quickly rot and kill the plants.

FLOWERING

Season   Flowers appear from mid- to late spring, the flowers completely covering the plant and hiding the foliage.

Cutting   The flowers are not suitable for picking.

AFTER FLOWERING

Requirements   It is probably easiest to shear radically over the whole plant with clippers, unless you are waiting for the seed to ripen. Shearing the plants also helps to keep a compact, neatly rounded shape.

BERGENIA
Elephant's ears

THE WELL-DEFINED, SOLID SHAPE of bergenias makes them ideal edging plants, as this neat row beside a path demonstrates. Bergenias have other advantages, too, in that they flower in the shade and from late winter on, both features that are not common among perennials.

FEATURES

SUMMER AUTUMN WINTER SPRING

EVERGREEN

An excellent evergreen, groundcover plant, also known as elephant's ears because of the large, rounded leaves about 20–30cm (8–12in) long. They are often leathery and glossy, generally green, many turning reddish in the autumn. The flowers are held on short stems, from mid-spring to early summer, some, such as 'Morgenrote', repeat flowering in cool conditions. The colour range is invariably shades of pink, with some white forms. Bergenia is not a fussy plant, and enjoys a wide range of conditions from bright sun to shade, from moist to dry ground. Long living and easy to propagate, it can colonise areas beneath trees, edge paths, or front a border.

BERGENIA AT A GLANCE

A versatile evergreen with large, ornamental foliage, that thrives in a range of conditions. Hardy to –18°C (0°F).

		RECOMMENDED VARIETIES
JAN	/	
FEB	flowering	*Bergenia* 'Abendglut'
MAR	flowering	B. 'Baby Doll'
APR	flowering	B. 'Bressingham Salmon'
MAY	flowering	B. 'Bressingham White'
JUN	/	B. *cordifolia* 'Purpurea'
JULY	/	B. 'Morgenrote'
AUG	/	B. *purpurescens*
SEPT	/	B. 'Silberlicht'
OCT	divide	
NOV	divide	
DEC	/	

CONDITIONS

Aspect Grows in either full sun or shady areas, but avoid extremes of the latter.

Site Likes well composted, moist soil with good drainage, but it will also tolerate much poorer conditions which brings out a richer winter leaf colour. Provide a late autumn mulch.

GROWING METHOD

Propagation Grows from seed sown in spring, producing hybrids, or divide in the spring or autumn every five years or so, to rejuvenate a declining plant. Plant up to 60cm (24in) apart, depending on the variety, or closer for immediate coverage.

Feeding Feed generously in early spring with a complete plant food, especially on poorer ground, and give a generous layer of mulch later in the autumn.

Problems Slugs and snails can be a major problem to the new young foliage, ruining its shapely appearance. Pick off, or treat with chemicals. Spray with a fungicide if leaf spot occurs.

FLOWERING

Season The flowers appear from late winter or early spring, depending on variety, for a few weeks.

Cutting Though the flowers are useful in cut flower arrangements, the foliage, especially when red in winter, makes a particularly attractive foil.

AFTER FLOWERING

Requirements Remove the spent flower stems and foliage.

CAMPANULA
Bellflower

CAMPANULA PERSICIFOLIA ALBA makes a valuable addition to a white border, flowering prolifically in early and mid-summer.

CAMPANULAS ARE THE MAINSTAY of the cottage or woodland garden, freely spreading, adding plenty of colour and charm.

FEATURES

HERBACEOUS

Also known as the bellflower, campanula contains about 300 species of annuals, biennials and perennials. Generally easy to grow in either full sun or dappled shade, on walls, banks and in borders, it has a wide range of flowers from the tubular to saucer-shaped. They also vary considerably in height from the low, 8cm (3in) high spreaders, like *C. betulifolia,* to the 1.5m (5ft) high *C. lactiflora*. The former are excellent at the front of a border, the latter need staking at the back. There are many excellent forms, *C. glomerata* 'Superba' is a vigorous grower, reaching 60 x 60cm (24 x 24in), while C. 'Burghaltii' produces pale lavender tubular bells around the same time.

CAMPANULA AT A GLANCE

A near 300-strong genus, thriving in a wide variety of conditions, grown for their abundant flowers. Hardy to −15°C (5°F).

		RECOMMENDED VARIETIES
JAN	/	
FEB	/	*Campanula arvatica*
MAR	sow	*C. carpatica*
APR	transplant	*C. garganica*
MAY	flowering	*C. latiloba*
JUN	flowering	*C. medium*
JULY	flowering	*C. persicifolia*
AUG	flowering	*C. thyrsoides*
SEPT	flowering	*C. trachelium*
OCT	divide	
NOV	/	
DEC	/	

CONDITIONS

Aspect   Campanula thrive in both sunny gardens and those with dappled shade.

Site   There are three broad types of campanula requiring different conditions: well-drained, fertile soil for border plants; moist, fast-draining ground for the rock garden species; and a gritty scree bed for the alpines that dislike being wet over winter.

GROWING METHOD

Propagation   Grow the species from seed in spring in a cold frame, or from cuttings, and sow alpines in a frame in autumn. Varieties must be propagated by spring cuttings, or spring or autumn division if they are to come true to the parent.

Feeding   Apply a complete plant food in spring, especially on poorer soils, or plenty of dug-in, organic material.

Problems   Slugs and snails are the major problem, and if not kept under control they can ruin a border display. In some areas *C. persicifolia* is prone to rust.

FLOWERING

Season   The long-lasting flowers appear from midwinter to spring.

Cutting   Makes an excellent display of cut flowers, especially the taller plants.

AFTER FLOWERING

Requirements Cut back to the ground in late autumn.

CENTRANTHUS RUBER
Red valerian

TRUSSES of rich crimson and softer pink valerian provide months of bright colour in the garden, rivalling the display of annuals.

RED VALERIAN flourishing in the conditions that suit it best – the fence provides shelter, and the raised bed warmth and good drainage.

FEATURES

This evergreen perennial is very easy to grow, but it often exceeds its allotted space by self-seeding (seedlings are easy to pull out). It has a long flowering period and can survive in poor, dry soil. It generally reaches 40cm (16in) high, but in good soil tops 70cm (28in). Flowers are a deep pink to red and there is a white form too. Ideal for a low-maintenance garden, it is often planted in mixed borders for its long display. It is also grown in large rockeries or on dry, fast-draining slopes. Self-sown plants can be found in almost no soil on rocky outcrops, and thrive in chalky ground.

CENTRANTHUS AT A GLANCE

C. ruber is a hardy, herbaceous perennial, a favourite in cottage gardens, with tall, red summer flowers. Hardy to −12°C (10°F).

		COMPANION PLANTS
JAN	/	
FEB	sow	*Argyranthemum foeniculaceum*
MAR	sow	*A. frutescens*
APR	transplant	Cytisus
MAY	transplant	*Geranium robertianum*
JUN	flowering	*Hedera colchica* 'Dentata
JULY	flowering	Variegata'
AUG	flowering	*Helleborus orientalis*
SEPT	flowering	Stipa
OCT	/	Yucca
NOV	/	
DEC	/	

CONDITIONS

Aspect	Likes full sun all day.
Soil	Needs very well-drained soil, but it need not be particularly rich.

GROWING METHOD

Propagation	Grows readily from tip cuttings taken in late spring and summer, or from seed sown in the spring. Space the plants 20cm (8in) apart.
Feeding	Fertiliser is generally not necessary, but you may give a little complete plant food in spring, as new growth begins. Needs regular water to establish, after which plants are extremely drought tolerant.
Problems	No specific problems are known.

FLOWERING

Season	The very long flowering period extends from spring until early autumn, especially if plants are cut back after each flowering flush to encourage plenty of new buds.
Cutting	Does not make a good cut flower.

AFTER FLOWERING

Requirements	No attention is needed beyond removing the spent flower stems. This has a double advantage: it keeps the plant looking neat, and prevents abundant self-seeding.

CHRYSANTHEMUM HYBRIDS
Dendranthema

THE QUILLED PETALS are characteristic of this open 'spider' style of chrysanthemum, as is the shading of colour.

HYBRID CHRYSANTHEMUMS are justifiably highly popular in the cut flower trade, and are available for most of the year.

CASCADING OVER the fence onto the massed erigeron below, this wonderful garden chrysanthemum gives a prolific display.

FEATURES

HERBACEOUS

Chrysanthemums probably originated in China, but were introduced into Japan a very long time ago. A big favourite in garden and florists' displays, they are the highlight of the late summer and autumn border. They are also widely used as a long-lasting cut flower. Chrysanthemums have been renamed and moved to the genus *Dendranthema*, though the name has yet to catch on. Four kinds to look out for include: the Korean (e.g. 'Yellow Starlet'), which give a long flowering performance but dislike excessive winter wet (store inside in severe conditions); the thigh-high, dwarf, bushy pompons ('Mei Kyo') with a sea of rounded flowers; the clump-forming rubellums (named hybrids of *C. rubellum*) which are hardiest, have a woody base, but again dislike extreme damp; and the sprays ('Pennine') which are grown both for the border and cutting.

Colour
The colour range is wide, covering white, cream, yellow, many shades of pink and lilac, burgundy, pale apricot and deep mahogany.

Types
There are many forms of chrysanthemums, and they have been classified by specialist societies and nurseries according to floral type. Some of the types are decorative, anemone centred, spider, pompon, single, exhibition, and Korean spray. There is virtually a shape for every taste.

Staking
Many of the taller varieties need staking, which needs to be carefully thought out if the display is to avoid looking too structured. One reliable, traditional method is to insert bamboo canes at intervals around and through the planting, and thread twine from cane to cane in a criss-cross fashion, perhaps 50–60cm (20–24in) above the ground.

CONDITIONS

Aspect
Grows best in full sun with protection from strong winds.

Site
Needs well-drained soil that has been heavily enriched with organic matter before planting. Plants should also be mulched with decayed compost or manure.

THIS UNUSUAL chrysanthemum has the central petals incurved like those of the Korean spray, while the outer ones are widespread.

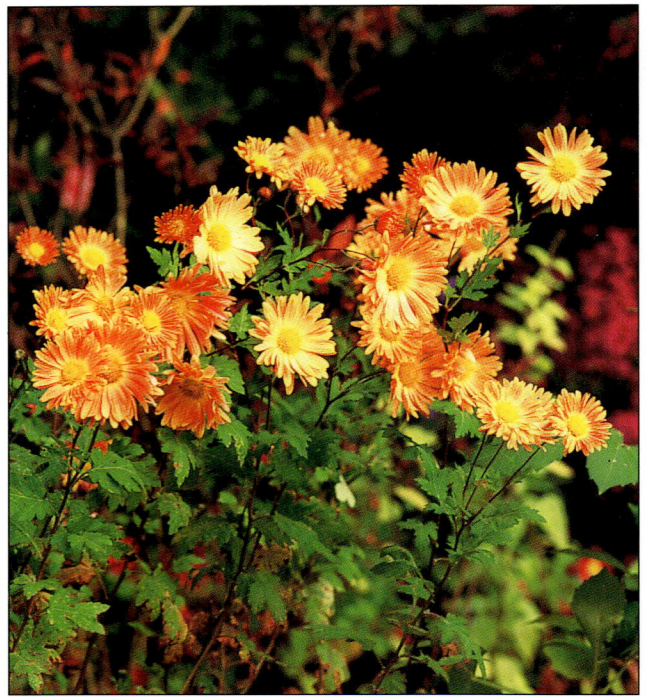

THE RUSSET COLOURS of these flowers seem appropriate to their autumn flowering season, when the leaves are turning.

GROWING METHOD

Propagation In spring lift and divide the new suckering growth so that each new plant has its own roots and shoots. Cuttings of the new growth can be taken. Space plants 40cm (16in) apart.

Feeding Once the plants are well established you can fertilise them every four to six weeks with a soluble liquid fertiliser.

Problems • You can spot chrysanthemum leaf miners by the wavy white or brown lines in the foliage. Furthermore, hold up the leaf to the light and you might see the pupa or grub. Control by immediately removing the affected leaves and crushing the grubs, or better still by regular spraying with a systemic insecticide.

• Chrysanthemum eelworm is evident by browning, drying leaves. Immediately destroy all infected plants. There is no available remedy.

• A number of fungal diseases can attack these plants, including leaf spot, powdery mildew, rust and white rust. Avoid overhead watering or watering late in the day, and ensure that residue from previous plantings is cleared away. You may need to spray with a registered fungicide. White rust is a particularly serious disease, and affected plants are probably best removed and destroyed.

• Watch for aphids clustering on new growth. Pick them off by hand, wash them off, or use an insecticidal spray.

CHRYSANTHEMUM AT A GLANCE

Chrysanthemums are the colourful mainstay of the the end-of-season border. The hardy forms will tolerate −15ºC (5ºF).

		RECOMMENDED VARIETIES
JAN	/	'Anna Marie'
FEB	sow	'Bronze Elegance'
MAR	sow	'Cappa'
APR	divide	'Faust'
MAY	transplant	'Lord Butler'
JUN	/	'Mrs Jessie Cooper'
JULY	/	'Poppet'
AUG	flowering	'Salmon Fairie'
SEPT	flowering	
OCT	/	
NOV	/	
DEC	/	

FLOWERING

Season Flowering time is mid- to late autumn. The exciting new race of Yoder or cushion chrysanthemums from America are dwarf, hardy, free-flowering (starting in late summer), and perfect for the front of the border. Those to look out for include 'Lynn', 'Robin', and 'Radiant Lynn'.

Cutting Cut flowers will last two to three weeks with frequent water changes, as long as the foliage is removed from the parts of the stems that are under water.

AFTER FLOWERING

Requirements Once flowering has finished, cut off plants 12.5–15cm (5–6in) above the ground.

CONVALLARIA
Lily-of-the-valley

LILY-OF-THE-VALLEY makes a vivid display because of the strong contrast between the shapely, oval leaves, and the small, bright white flowers. It can be left to naturalise in woodland conditions, or allowed to spread through a shady border. Though invasive, it is quite easily controlled.

FEATURES

HERBACEOUS

Lily-of-the-valley is a one species (sometimes considered three) genus, featuring the bell-shaped, fragrant *Convallaria majalis*. A native of Europe, it grows in woods and meadows, and produces 20cm (8in) tall stems of nodding white flowers shortly after the foliage has unfurled. Given the right conditions, namely a cool, moist area, it can spread extremely quickly by means of underground shoots, but it is easily controlled. There are several attractive forms, 'Albostriata' having cream striped foliage, and 'Fortin's Giant' flowers up to 15mm ($\frac{1}{2}$in) across. Lily-of-the-valley is essential in a woodland area, or in a damp shady spot where little else of note will grow.

CONVALLARIA AT A GLANCE

Basically a one-species genus with wonderful, waxy, scented spring flowers. Hardy to −15°C (5°F). Good cultivars available.

		COMPANION PLANTS
JAN	/	
FEB	/	Bergenia
MAR	/	*Euphorbia robbiae*
APR	transplant	Galanthus
MAY	flowering	Primula
JUN	/	Pulmonaria
JULY	/	Rodgersia
AUG	sow	
SEPT	division	
OCT	division	
NOV	/	
DEC	/	

CONDITIONS

Aspect   Shade is essential.
Site   The soil must be damp, rich and leafy. For an impressive, vigorous display, apply a thick mulch of leaf mould around the clumps of plants every autumn.

GROWING METHOD

Propagation   When the seed is ripe remove the fleshy covering, and raise in a cold frame. Alternatively, divide the rhizomes in the autumn. A 15cm (6in) piece will provide approximately six new plants. The success rate is generally high. Make sure that young plants are not allowed to dry out. Mulch them to guarantee against moisture loss.
Feeding   Every other year apply a scattering of complete fertiliser in the spring.
Problems   *Botrytis* can be a problem, but is rarely anything to worry about.

FLOWERING

Season   One brief display in late spring.
Cutting   Lily-of-the-valley makes excellent cut flowers, providing a striking spring display, while emitting a gentle sweet scent. They can also be lifted and grown indoors in a pot to flower the following spring. When finished, replace in the garden.

AFTER FLOWERING

Requirements   Remove the spent flower stems, but leave the foliage intact to provide the energy for next year's display.

COREOPSIS
Coreopsis

COREOPSIS ARE *wonderful plants which can quickly colonise a space, say between shrubs, producing striking, bright yellow flowers.*

THIS DOUBLE-FLOWERED FORM *of golden coreopsis provides many weeks of marvellous colour throughout the summer.*

FEATURES

HERBACEOUS

SUMMER AUTUMN WINTER SPRING

Perennial coreopsis carries a profusion of bright yellow daisy-like flowers over a long period, generally through summer into the autumn, though some do flower in spring. Regular deadheading will ensure a long display. *C. lanceolata*, known as calliopsis, has become naturalised in many parts of the world. The strong-growing *C. grandiflora* may grow 60–90cm (24–36in) high, with C.*verticillata* about 20cm (8in) shorter. There are several species worth trying, some with dwarf form or flowers displaying a dark eye. The foliage is variable, too. The plants are easy to grow. Plant in bold clumps in a mixed border.

COREOPSIS AT A GLANCE

A genus with well over 100 species that make a big contribution to the summer and early autumn display. Hardy to –15° (5°C).

		RECOMMENDED VARIETIES
JAN	/	*Coreopsis auriculata*
FEB	/	'Schnittgold'
MAR	/	C. 'Goldfink'
APR	sow	C. *grandiflora* 'Early Sunrise'
MAY	divide	C. *g.* 'Mayfield Giant'
JUN	flowering	'Sunray'
JULY	flowering	C. *verticillata*
AUG	flowering	C. *v.* 'Grandiflora'
SEPT	flowering	C. *v.* 'Zagreb'
OCT	/	
NOV	/	
DEC	/	

CONDITIONS

Aspect Prefers an open, sunny position right through the day, with little shade.

Site Performs best in well-drained soil enriched with organic matter, but it will grow in poor soils too. Over-rich soil may produce a profusion of foliage with poor flowering.

GROWING METHOD

Propagation Grows most easily from divisions of existing clumps lifted in the spring. Space new plants at about 30cm (12in) intervals. Species can be grown from seed sown in mid-spring. Since cultivars of *C. grandiflora* can be ephemeral, sow seed for continuity.

Feeding Apply complete plant food as growth begins in the spring. However, no further feeding should be needed.

Problems No pest or disease problems are known.

FLOWERING

Season The long flowering period extends through summer and autumn. *C.* 'Early Sunrise', C.*lanceolata*, and 'Sunray' flower in their first year from an early sowing.

Cutting Flowers can be cut for indoor decoration.

AFTER FLOWERING

Requirements Cut off spent flower stems and tidy up the foliage as it dies back. In mild, frost-free winters coreopsis may not totally die back.

CORYDALIS
Corydalis

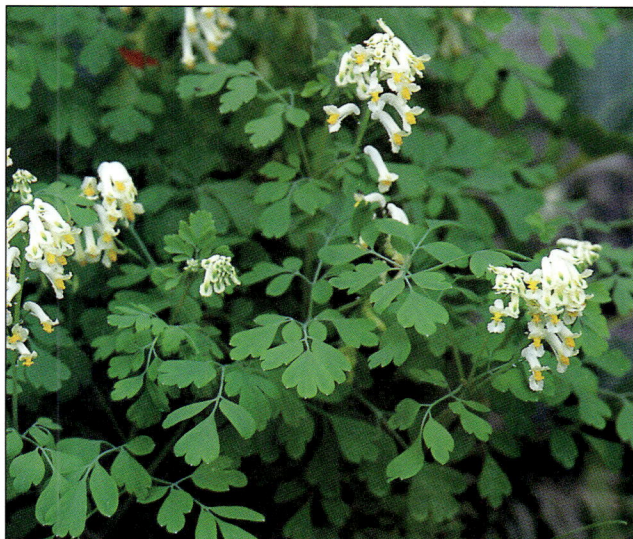

THE FOLIAGE *and flowers of* Corydalis ochroleuca *are dainty and highly decorative. Looks good in walls and ornamental pots.*

THE BLUE SPECIES *and forms of corydalis are highly prized. This is* Corydalis flexuosa *with long, upcurving spurs on its flowers.*

FEATURES

HERBACEOUS

Pretty, fern-like foliage and tubular, spurred flowers are characteristic of the 300 or so species of corydalis. Only a small number of species are actually grown in cultivation, and they mainly flower in shades of yellow or blue, but there are some in pink or crimson. Some of the brilliant blues make a distinctive feature, and a recent cultivar with electric blue flowers, known as *C. flexuosa* 'China Blue', is now widely available. It mixes well with *C. solida* 'George Baker', salmon-pink, and *C. ochroleuca*, white. Heights vary from 15–60cm (6–24in). Many corydalis are excellent rock garden plants, while others are suitable for mixed borders or planting under deciduous trees. Many varieties may be available only from specialist nurseries growing alpine plants.

CORYDALIS AT A GLANCE

A large group of annuals, biennials, and perennials, growing in a wide range of moist and dry conditions. Hardy to –15ºC (5ºF).

JAN	/	
FEB	/	**RECOMMENDED VARIETIES**
MAR	/	*Corydalis cashmeriana*
APR	divide	*C. cava*
MAY	transplant	*C. cheilanthifolia*
JUN	flowering	*C. elata*
JULY	flowering	*C.lutea*
AUG	flowering	*C.sempervirens*
SEPT	divide	*C. solida*
OCT	sow	*C. s.* 'Beth Evans'
NOV	/	*C. s. f. transsylvanica*
DEC	/	*C. s. f.* 'George Baker'

CONDITIONS

Aspect   The preferred aspect varies with the species. Some tolerate an open, sunny position, while others need degrees of dappled sunlight. Species grown in 'hot spots' should be given plenty of shade.

Site   Needs very well-drained soil that is able to retain some moisture in summer.

GROWING METHOD

Propagation   Grows from seed sown as soon as it is ripe, in the autumn. The seed is ripe when the small elongated capsules, which form after the flowers have fallen, turn brown and dry. Some species can be divided, while others produce tubers from which offsets can be taken. Plant at approximate 10–15cm (4–6in) intervals. New young plants need regular watering in prolonged, dry weather during the spring and summer months.

Feeding   Apply a sprinkling of slow-release fertiliser as growth commences in the spring.

Problems   There are no specific pest or disease problems.

FLOWERING

Season   Most species flower in spring, or from spring into summer. *C. flexuosa* dies down in the summer.

Cutting   The flowers are unsuitable for cutting.

AFTER FLOWERING

Requirements   Remove spent flower stems unless you are waiting for seed to set. Tidy up the foliage as it dies back.

CYNARA CARDUNCULUS

Cardoon

CARDOON LOOKS *rather like a Scotch thistle. Its purple flowers can be left to dry, and then used for a striking indoor arrangement.*

THE SILVERY LEAVES *of cardoon are distinctive, large and shapely, and a big clump provides a geometric, sculptural feature.*

FEATURES

SUMMER AUTUMN WINTER SPRING

HERBACEOUS

A close relative of the globe artichoke, the cardoon is generally grown for its arching, 1m (39in) long, silver-grey foliage. Growing up to 2m (78in) high and almost 2m (78in) wide, it is a terrific accent plant for the back of a border, or it can be combined with low-growing green plants in an open position. Both the colour and form stand out against most other plants. The purple, thistle-like flowers develop in summer, and the dried heads left on the plant make a decorative autumn feature. Cardoon is edible, being grown for the tasty, fleshy base of each leaf. It is difficult to place in a small garden since you need room to stand back and appreciate its startling form.

CYNARA AT A GLANCE

C. cardunculus is a clump-forming perennial grown for its long, striking foliage and purple flowers. Hardy to −18°C (0°F).

		Companion Plants
Jan	/	
Feb	/	Brugmansia
Mar	sow	Centranthus
Apr	divide	Echinops
May	transplant	Geranium
Jun	flowering	Miscanthus
July	flowering	Rose
Aug	flowering	Salvia
Sept	flowering	Yucca
Oct	/	
Nov	/	
Dec	/	

CONDITIONS

Aspect   Needs full sun all day for best results. Also needs shelter from strong, leaf-tearing winds.

Soil   Needs rich, well-drained soil. Before planting, dig in large amounts of manure or compost.

GROWING METHOD

Propagation   Propagate in late spring, or grow from seed. Position plants at least 1.2m (4ft) apart. Seed-grown plants are variable in quality, and do not normally reach maturity in their first year. During the growing season regular, deep watering is essential for new, young plants in prolonged, dry spells.

Feeding   Apply a complete plant food as growth commences in the spring, and repeat mid-summer. When cardoon is grown as a vegetable it is given a weekly liquid feed.

Problems   Beware of the sharp points on the flowerheads.

FLOWERING

Season   The purple, thistle-like flowers appear during summer on stems 2–3m (6½–10ft) high.

Cutting   If the flowers are allowed to dry on the plant, they can be cut and used as part of a big, bold indoor decoration.

AFTER FLOWERING

Requirements   Once the flowers have lost their decorative value, cut off the whole stem low down. As the plant starts to die off and look tatty, cut it back just above the ground.

DELPHINIUM
Delphinium

DOZENS OF individual flowers make up the striking spires of the delphinium. Blue shades, from pale to purple, predominate.

THESE STAKED DELPHINIUMS, growing in the shelter of a house, should remain stately and upright through the flowering season.

FEATURES

SUMMER AUTUMN WINTER SPRING

HERBACEOUS

Tall, handsome and stately, delphiniums make an outstanding feature in perennial borders. Growing from 1–2m 39–78in) high, the long-lasting spires of blooms originally came in a rich blue only, but now offer shades of pink, lavender, white and red. Delphiniums should be mass planted at the back of a border for the best effect, but they can also be placed as accent plants at intervals across a border. They mix well with climbers like clematis. Tall-growing varieties may need staking unless they are in a very sheltered spot. Colours can be mixed, but the best effect comes from massing plants of the same colour.

DELPHINIUM AT A GLANCE

A hardy annual, biennial and perennial it is grown for its striking, vertical spires, thick with flowers. Hardy to −15°C (5°F).

Month	Activity		RECOMMENDED VARIETIES
Jan	/		
Feb	sow		*Delphinium* 'Bruce'
Mar	sow		'Cassius'
Apr	transplant		'Emily Hawkins'
May	transplant		'Lord Butler'
Jun	flowering		'Our Deb'
July	flowering		'Rosemary Brock'
Aug	flowering		'Sandpiper'
Sept	/		'Sungleam'
Oct	divide		'Walton Gemstone'
Nov	/		
Dec	/		

CONDITIONS

Aspect Needs full sun and shelter from strong winds, and staking if not well sheltered.

Soil Needs well-drained soil enriched with copious amounts of decayed manure or compost before planting. Water regularly and mulch.

GROWING METHOD

Propagation Divide established clumps in the autumn, ensuring each division has a crown and its own roots. Space about 30cm (12in) apart. Grows from seed sown in spring, but the results are variable. Take 8cm (3in) basal cuttings in mid-spring.

Feeding Apply complete plant food once growth begins in the spring, and each month until flowering.

Problems Watch for aphids on new growth, and hose off or spray with pyrethrum or insecticidal soap. In humid conditions a bad attack of powdery mildew may need to be tackled by spraying with a fungicide. Beware slugs.

FLOWERING

Season Blooms for a long season through early and late summer.

Cutting Flowers make a good display, and can be dried.

AFTER FLOWERING

Requirements Remove the flower stems when the main blooms fade and small spikes may flower in late summer and early autumn.

DIANTHUS CARYOPHYLLUS
Wild carnation

FRINGED PINK FLOWERS and silver-grey buds and stems make this a classic.

UPWARD-ANGLED CANES are one way of making sure that top-heavy blooms do not tumble onto a path. The other, more discrete method is to employ a series of small twiggy sticks.

FEATURES

SUMMER AUTUMN WINTER SPRING
EVERGREEN

Carnations are very popular both as cut flowers and as a garden subject. Flowers are carried singly or in groups on stems 30–50cm (12–20in) high, although florists' carnations may be taller. *Dianthus caryophyllus* from the Mediterranean, a woody perennial with elegant stiff stems, bears richly scented, purple-pink flowers which grow taller than the average, reaching 80cm (32in) under perfect conditions. It has given rise to several excellent series. The Floristan Series comes in a wide colour range, and makes good cut flowers, the Knight Series is shorter and bushier, and includes yellow, white and orange, and the Lilliput Series, shorter still at 20cm (8in), includes a rich scarlet.

DIANTHUS AT A GLANCE

D. caryophyllus is a colourful woody perennial, part of the large dianthus family of over 300 species. Hardy to –15°C (5°F).

		COMPANION PLANTS
JAN	/	
FEB	/	
MAR	sow	Campanula
APR	/	Cistus
MAY	transplant	Crepis
JUN	flowering	Eryngium
JULY	flowering	Helianthemum
AUG	flowering	Portulaca
SEPT	/	Sedum
OCT	/	Tulip
NOV	/	
DEC	sow	

CONDITIONS

Aspect   Needs full sun all day. Protect from very strong winds.

Soil   Needs very well-drained soil with plenty of additional, well-decayed organic matter. Unless the soil is alkaline, apply a light dressing of lime before each planting.

GROWING METHOD

Propagation   Grows easily from cuttings taken at almost any time. Use leafy side shoots and strip off all but the top leaves. Roots form in 3–5 weeks. Space newly rooted plants 20cm (8in) apart. Water regularly to establish, then occasionally in dry weather. Carnations tolerate dry conditions well.

Feeding   Little fertiliser is needed if the soil contains plenty of organic matter, but you may give a complete feed twice – in spring and again in mid-summer.

Problems   Carnation rust, a fungal disease, is common in warm, humid conditions. Greyish spots appear on leaves or stems, and the foliage may curl and yellow. Take prompt action by immediately spraying with a fungicide. Squash caterpillars when seen.

FLOWERING

Season   The crop of flowers appears in summer, but it can be forced for other times. Remove any excess buds to produce good-sized, main blooms.

Cutting   An excellent cut flower. Recut stems between nodes (joints) to aid water uptake.

DIANTHUS CULTIVARS
Pinks

DIANTHUS CULTIVARS make reliable, popular edging plants with bright colours and, in many cases, a rich, pervasive scent.

ONE OF THE BEST pinks for the garden, or as a cut flower, 'Doris' is vigorous, long flowering and sweetly scented. A 'must'.

FEATURES

SUMMER AUTUMN WINTER SPRING
EVERGREEN

Pinks are crosses of *D. caryophyllus* (wild carnation) and *D. plumarius* (cottage pink). Allwood Brothers nursery in West Sussex has bred an enormous range of cultivars that are free flowering given the right conditions. The grey-green foliage grows in a tufted mat and flowering stems are 10–30cm (4–12in) high. Most flowers are heavily scented and may be single or bicoloured, some with a clear margin of contrasting colour. Most are white, pink, red, deep crimson or salmon, with cultivars ideally suited for the rock garden.

CONDITIONS

Aspect   Needs full sun all day, and protection from strong winds.
Site   Needs very free-draining soil, enriched with

additional decayed organic matter, well ahead of planting. Use a soil-testing kit to determine whether your soil is acid – if so, add quantities of lime according to the manufacturer's instructions. Beware of exceeding the recommended rate, it will simply do more harm than good.

GROWING METHOD

Propagation   Grows easily from cuttings taken in late summer and autumn. Start fresh plants every three or four years to keep vigorous compact growth. Space the plant approximately 15–30cm (6–12in) apart, depending on variety. Water until the plants are well established.
Feeding   Apply complete plant food in early spring, as active spring growth begins.
Problems   Aphids and slugs are the two major problems. The former can be tackled by a regular spraying programme with, for example, malathion. The latter can be spotted late at night or early in the morning. Either treat chemically, or pick off by hand and drown.

FLOWERING

Season   Some pinks flower during spring only, others have a long flowering period from spring to early autumn.
Cutting   Pinks make excellent cut flowers, providing indoor decoration and scent.

AFTER FLOWERING

Requirements   Cut off any spent flower stems to the ground as they fade. No other pruning action is necessary.

DIANTHUS AT A GLANCE

The cultivars include perennials in a wide colour range, many richly scented. Generally hardy to –15°C (5°F).

JAN	/	**RECOMMENDED VARIETIES**
FEB	/	
MAR	sow	*Dianthus alpinus*
APR	transplant	'Bovey Belle'
MAY	transplant	'Devon Glow'
JUN	flowering	*D. deltoides*
JULY	flowering	'La Bourboule'
AUG	flowering	'Monica Wyatt'
SEPT	/	'Sam Barlow'
OCT	sow	'Whitehill'
NOV	/	'Widecombe Fair'
DEC	/	

DIASCIA
Twinspur

ONE OF THE MOST USEFUL garden plants, twinspur flowers right through the season, from spring to autumn. And being 30cm (12in) high, it makes the perfect front-of-border filler, tolerating a sunny position, and one with a degree of shade. Despite a short lifespan, it is easily propagated.

FEATURES

Twinspur has an extremely long flowering season, lasting from spring until the first frosts. Though there is a large number of forms available, ranging from 'Lilac Mist' to 'Salmon Supreme', the colour range is quite limited, essentially being shades of pink. Diascia requires moist, rich soil, but over-feeding will result in fewer flowers. The height ranges from 15–30cm (6–12in), which means the taller plants can be given free reign to burst through their neighbours, adding to the display. 'Salmon Supreme' is an attractive low-spreader, being 15cm (6in) high. *D. vigilis* is twice as tall, hardier, and even more free flowering.

DIASCIA AT A GLANCE

A near 50-strong genus of annuals and perennials, with a pink colour and a long flowering season. Hardy to –5°C (23°F).

		RECOMMENDED VARIETIES
JAN	/	*Diascia barberae* 'Ruby
FEB	sow	Field'
MAR	divide	*D.* 'Dark Eyes'
APR	transplant	*D.* 'Hector's Hardy'
MAY	flowering	*D. integerrima*
JUN	flowering	*D.* 'Lilac Mist'
JULY	flowering	*D.* 'Rupert Lambert'
AUG	flowering	*D. vigilis*
SEPT	flowering	
OCT	/	
NOV	/	
DEC	/	

CONDITIONS

Aspect   Enjoys full sun; though it tolerates some shade it will not flower as long or as prolifically.
Soil   Moisture-retentive, well-drained ground.

GROWING METHOD

Propagation   This is essential since diascias are short-lived, but propagation is easily managed. Success rates are high by all methods, though cuttings are particularly easy. Either sow seed when ripe, or the following spring, take cuttings during the growing season, or divide in spring. Since young plants might die in severe winters, keep indoor cuttings as possible replacements.
Feeding   Mulch well in the spring to enrich the soil.
Problems   Slugs and snails are the main enemies. Pick them off or use a chemical treatment.

FLOWERING

Season   An unusually long season from spring, beyond the end of summer to the first frosts.
Cutting   Diascias cut well, and though they do not last particularly long in water, replacements are quickly available fom the parent plant.

AFTER FLOWERING

Requirements   Cut ruthlessly to the ground after flowering to promote a second flush of flowers.

DICENTRA SPECTABILIS
Bleeding heart

THE ARCHING STEMS of this bleeding heart carry masses of bright pink, heart-shaped flowers resembling tiny lockets.

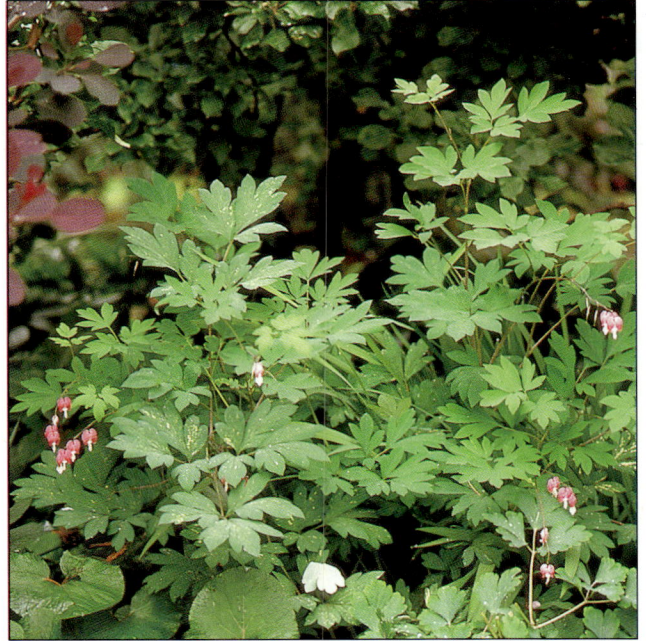

THE BLEEDING HEART is well worth growing for its foliage alone as the delicate, fern-like leaves are very decorative.

FEATURES

HERBACEOUS

With fern-like foliage and curving stems bearing pretty pink and white, heart-shape flowers, bleeding heart is an all-time favourite perennial. It appeals to children and adults alike. There is a cultivar, 'Alba', which has pure white flowers. Another species less commonly grown is *D. formosa*, which has very ferny foliage, but its flowers are not so completely heart-shaped. Bleeding heart can be grown in a mixed border or in the filtered shade of trees. Plants may reach 40–60cm (16–24in) high in good conditions, and form a clump 50cm (20in) or so wide.

DICENTRA AT A GLANCE

D. spectabilis is a clump-forming perennial, with arching stems and decorative deep pink flowers. Hardy to −18°C (0°F).

Month	Activity		RECOMMENDED VARIETIES
Jan	/		
Feb	/		*D.* 'Adrian Bloom'
Mar	sow		'Bountiful'
Apr	transplant		*D. cucularia*
May	transplant		*D. f. alba*
Jun	flowering		'Langtrees'
July	flowering		'Ruby Slippers'
Aug	/		*D. macrantha*
Sept	/		*D. spectabilis*
Oct	division		*D. s.* 'Alba'
Nov	sow		'Stuart Boothman'
Dec	/		

CONDITIONS

Aspect Grows best in filtered sunlight. Strong, hot, drying winds make it shrivel up. A sheltered position protects against late frosts.

Site Needs well-drained soil rich in organic matter. Dig in copious quantities of decayed manure or compost several weeks before planting.

GROWING METHOD

Propagation Divide large established clumps in the autumn, and plant divisions 25–30cm (10–12in) apart. Also grows from seed sown in the spring or autumn. Needs regular, deep watering during dry periods in spring and summer.

Feeding Apply a sprinkling of a complete plant food whenever growth begins in the spring.

Problems There are no specific pest or disease problems known for this plant.

FLOWERING

Season Blooms for several weeks during late spring and early summer.

Cutting Flowers are not suitable for cutting.

AFTER FLOWERING

Requirements Cut out spent flower stems. As the foliage yellows and dies off, cut it off just above the ground.

DIGITALIS
Foxglove

A SUPERB DISPLAY of Digitalis grandiflora, *the yellow foxglove, which sends up 1m (39in) high spires. It is an excellent choice for gaps towards the back of the border, though you may well have to weed out some seedlings that spread beyond the main clump.*

FEATURES

HERBACEOUS

Foxgloves are essentials for the cottage garden, self-seeding in unexpected places, with their tall spires of often richly coloured flowers. They grow in most soils and situations, from the shady to sunny, and dryish to damp, though performance is variable at these extremes. They also make a large group of biennials and perennials ranging in height from 60cm–2m (24in–6½ft). The common foxglove (*D. purpurea)* can be grown as a perennial, but its lifespan is short, the biennial generally being the preferred option. The colour range includes red, yellow, white and pink with the early summer Fox Hybrids. *D. grandiflora* has the largest flowers.

DIGITALIS AT A GLANCE

Foxgloves are grown for their tall spires of attractive, tubular flowers, generally in soft hues. Hardy to −15°C (5°F).

JAN	/	
FEB	/	
MAR	sow	
APR	transplant	
MAY	transplant	
JUN	flowering	
JULY	flowering	
AUG	/	
SEPT	/	
OCT	/	
NOV	/	
DEC	/	

RECOMMENDED VARIETIES

Digitalis ferruginea

D. grandiflora

D. lanata

D. parviflora

D. purpurea

D. p. Excelsior Group

CONDITIONS

Aspect Dappled shade for part of the day is ideal, but it is not absolutely essential. Foxgloves are undemanding plants, and will grow in a wide range of gardens.

Site The soil conditions can vary, but humus-rich ground gives the best results.

GROWING METHOD

Propagation Sow seed of new varieties in containers, in a cold frame, in late spring. Space seedlings up to 45cm (18in) apart. If you already have some plants it is not necessary since the foxglove is a prolific self-seeder. Dig up a new plant and transplant to where it is required. Water in well, and do not let it dry out.

Feeding Provide a complete feed in the spring. In particularly dry soil provide a protective spring mulch.

Problems Leaf spot and powdery mildew can strike, spraying being the best treatment.

FLOWERING

Season Flowers appear in early and mid-summer.

Cutting While they make good cut flowers, handle with extreme caution. The foliage can irritate the skin, and all parts are poisonous.

AFTER FLOWERING

Requirements Leave just a few stems to seed where the foxgloves look good, mixing well with other plants, otherwise deadhead to avoid masses of invasive seedlings.

ECHINACEA PURPUREA

Purple coneflower

BOLDER THAN many perennials, coneflowers are sometimes slow to appear in spring but they are definitely well worth the wait.

THIS FINE STAND of bright purple coneflowers adds a striking touch to this scheme. The flowers fade as they age, but petals don't fall.

FEATURES

HERBACEOUS

Native to the prairie states of the United States, the coneflower is a hardy, drought-resistant plant. Its dark, cone-shape centre is surrounded by rich pink ray petals, and there are cultivars available in shades of pink-purple and white. They make excellent cut flowers. Coneflowers often grow over 1m (39in) high, and are a great addition to a perennial border because they bloom over a long period from mid-summer into autumn, when many other plants have finished. Ideally Echinacea should be mass planted to get the best effect. Excellent varieties include *E. purpurea* Bressingham Hybrids, 'Magnus', and 'White Swan'.

ECHINACEA AT A GLANCE

E. purpurea is an attractive, daisy-like perennial with purple flowers, ideal for naturalising or borders. Hardy to −15°C (5°F).

		COMPANION PLANTS
JAN	/	
FEB	sow	Allium
MAR	sow	Delphinium
APR	transplant	Geranium
MAY	transplant	Gladiolus
JUN	/	Iris
JULY	flowering	Lavandula
AUG	flowering	Rosemary
SEPT	flowering	Yucca
OCT	divide	Delphinium
NOV	/	Rose
DEC	/	

CONDITIONS

Aspect   Prefers full sun all day. Although it is tolerant of windy conditions, the blooms will have a better appearance if the plants are sheltered from strong winds.

Site   Needs well-drained, rich soil. Poor or sandy soils can be improved by digging in large quantities of compost or manure before planting.

GROWING METHOD

Propagation   Divide existing clumps in early spring or autumn, and replant divisions 20–25cm (8–10in) apart. It can be grown from seed sown in early spring, which may produce colour variations. Needs regular water to establish in prolonged dry spells, but occasional deep soakings in dry weather are enough, as it tolerates dry conditions well.

Feeding   Apply complete plant food in early spring and again in mid-summer.

Problems   No specific problems are known.

FLOWERING

Season   There is a long flowering period from late summer into autumn.

Cutting   Cut flowers for the vase when fully open, but before the petals separate out.

AFTER FLOWERING

Requirements   Remove spent flower stems. The whole plant can be cut back to ground level in winter.

ECHINOPS
Globe thistle

THESE METALLIC BLUE globe thistles form an elegant picture against a stone wall.

EARLY MORNING LIGHT accentuates the rounded, slightly spiky heads of these globe thistle flowers, planted here in a bold drift in a country garden.

FEATURES

SUMMER AUTUMN WINTER SPRING

HERBACEOUS

This is a very distinctive looking plant that makes a good accent in a mixed planting. Taller species need to be placed at the back of a border, but others can be planted in bold groups through the bed. Most have foliage that is stiff, prickly and finely divided, with silvery stems growing from 30cm–2m (12in–6½ft). Some of the species have foliage that is covered with fine white hairs on the underside. The flowerheads are usually white or metallic blue, and are highly prized for their decorative value when cut and dried. The most commonly grown is *E. ritro* and its cultivars, some of which have deep blue flowers. *E. sphaerocephalus* has pale grey to silvery flowers.

ECHINOPS AT A GLANCE

A group of annuals, biennials and perennials grown for their geometric shapes and blue flowers. Hardy to –5/10°C (23°/5°F).

JAN	divide	
FEB	divide	
MAR	sow	
APR	/	
MAY	transplant	
JUN	/	
JULY	flowering	
AUG	flowering	
SEPT	flowering	
OCT	divide	
NOV	divide	

RECOMMENDED VARIETIES

Echinops bannaticus 'Blue Globe'

E. b. 'Taplow Blue'

E. ritro ruthenicus

E. r. Veitch's Blue'

COMPANION PLANTS

Buddleja

Kniphofia

Perovskia

CONDITIONS

Aspect   Prefers full sun all day.
Site   Soil must be very well drained but need not be rich. The globe thistle can be grown in poor, gravel-like or sandy soils.

GROWING METHOD

Propagation   It can either be grown from seed, from division of existing clumps, or from root cuttings. All propagation is done from autumn to winter. Plant out about 40cm (16in) apart. Water regularly to establish. Although drought tolerant, this plant benefits from occasional deep watering during prolonged dry spring and summer periods.
Feeding   Apply a complete plant food or poultry manure in early spring.
Problems   There are no known pest or disease problems, but plants will rot on sticky clay or poorly drained soil.

FLOWERING

Season   Each species or variety will flower for approximately two months.
Cutting   Flowerheads required for drying should be cut before the blooms are fully open.

AFTER FLOWERING

Requirements   Cut off any remaining spent flowerheads unless you want the seed to ripen. As the plant dies down, clean away dead foliage wearing gloves to protect against the foliage.

EPIMEDIUM
Barrenwort / Bishop's mitre

NEW GROWTH on the bishop's mitre bears attractive bronze or pink shadings, but the older foliage is plain green.

A DENSE CARPET of bishop's mitre makes a wonderful groundcover under a grove of shapely Japanese maples.

FEATURES

HERBACEOUS

EVERGREEN

This low-growing perennial is grown more for its attractive foliage than its flowers, although the flowers are quite attractive. The shape resembles a bishop's mitre, giving rise to its common name. Many species have small, starry flowers in white, cream or yellow, although there are pale and rose-pink varieties too. This is a woodland plant which makes a good groundcover or filler for shady parts of the garden. Some die down completely in winter, while others remain evergreen. Plants are rarely more than 30cm (12in) tall. Combine it with plants such as Solomon's seal, primrose or lenten rose, which enjoy similar woodland-type conditions.

EPIMEDIUM AT A GLANCE

An evergreen, deciduous perennial making excellent groundcover in shady situations. Small flowers. Hardy to –15°C (5°F).

		RECOMMENDED VARIETIES
JAN	/	
FEB	sow	*Epimedium cantabrigiense*
MAR	/	*E. grandiflorum*
APR	transplant	*E. g.* 'Nanum'
MAY	flowering	*E. g.* "Rose Queen'
JUN	/	*E. perralderianum*
JULY	/	*E. pinnatum colchicum*
AUG	/	*E.* x *rubrum*
SEPT	sow	*E.* x *versicolor* 'Sulphureum'
OCT	divide	
NOV	/	
DEC	/	

CONDITIONS

Aspect   Needs dappled shade with protection from strong winds.

Site   Needs well-drained soil heavily enriched with organic matter. Regular mulching is beneficial to retain moisture.

GROWING METHOD

Propagation   Clumps can be divided in the autumn although with some varieties this is not easy. Pull apart or cut away sections of plant, keeping both roots and a bud or shoot on each piece. Plant 15–20cm (6–8in) apart. Some species seed readily. Keep young plants well watered until well established.

Feeding   Apply a slow-release fertiliser in the spring.

Problems   Snails may attack soft new growth as it appears, so take precautions.

FLOWERING

Season   The small flowers appear in spring along with the leaves. But shear off the foliage of all varieties in winter even when green (except *E. perralderianum),* to prevent the flowers being hidden. Fresh leaves will quickly follow.

Cutting   Flowers can be cut for the vase and last quite well in water.

AFTER FLOWERING

Requirements Spent flower stems can be clipped off. Old, dead foliage should be tidied up and removed by the end of autumn.

ERYNGIUM
Sea holly

AN OUTSTANDING PLANT for the Mediterranean garden is Eryngium maritimum. *It has strong architectural features with a stiff, branching habit, and mid- to late summer flowers. It can be grown in the border, or better still in a gravel bed to highlight the shape.*

FEATURES

HERBACEOUS

EVERGREEN

Sea holly is a 230-species strong genus, with annuals, biennials and perennials. Though they are related to cow parsley they bear no resemblance, being grown for their marvellous, attractive, spikey appearance, blue flowers (though some are white or green), and ability to thrive in poor, rocky, sunny ground. Heights can vary considerably from *E. alpinum,* 70cm (28in) tall, which as its name suggests grows in the Alps, to *E. eburneum* from South America which can reach 1.5m (5ft), and *E. pandanifolium* which is much taller at 3m (10ft). One of the most attractive is the Moroccan *E. variifolium* which has rounded, white-veined foliage setting off the pale blue

ERYNGIUM AT A GLANCE

Annuals, and deciduous/evergreen perennials grown for their shape. Hardiness varies from −10°C (13°F) to −18°C (0°F).

		RECOMMENDED VARIETIES
JAN	/	
FEB	sow	*Eryngium alpinum*
MAR	division	*E. a.* 'Blue Star'
APR	transplant	*E. bourgatii*
MAY	transplant	*E. b.* 'Oxford Blue'
JUN	flowering	*E. giganteum*
JULY	flowering	*E. x oliverianum*
AUG	flowering	*E. x tripartitum*
SEPT	flowering	
OCT	sow	
NOV	/	
DEC	/	

flowers. It is also more manageable at 35cm (14in) high – good for the front of a border.

CONDITIONS

Aspect Grow in full sun, well out of the shade.
Site There are two types of sea holly, with different growing needs. Most prefer fast-draining, fertile ground (e.g. *E. alpinum* and *E. bourgatii),* and some (e.g. *E. eburneum*) poor stoney ground, out of the winter wet.

GROWING METHOD

Propagation Sow the seed when ripe; alternatively take root cuttings in late winter, or divide in the spring.
Feeding Only for the first kind of sea holly which benefits from a spring feed, and some well-rotted manure. Good drainage is important.
Problems Slugs and snails are the main problem when sea holly is grown in the border, damaging the new young leaves. Promptly remove when seen, or use a chemical treatment.

FLOWERING

Season The earliest sea hollies begin flowering in early summer, while others last from mid- to early or mid-autumn in dry weather.
Cutting Sea holly makes an invaluable cut flower. They also make exceptional dried arrangements, combining with other architectural plants and softer, flowery ones.

AFTER FLOWERING

Requirements Cut back the spent flowering stems to the ground.

EUPHORBIA
Spurge

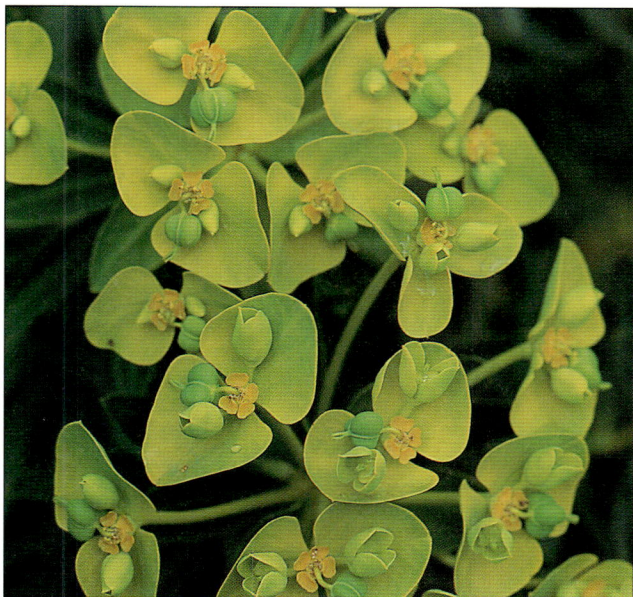

THE HIGHLY VERSATILE spurge tolerates a wide range of conditions. One of its chief attractions is its striking bracts.

A MIXED BORDER showing the value of propagating your own euphorbia. Strong shapes, flowing clumps, it even thrives in the shade.

FEATURES

HERBACEOUS

EVERGREEN

A large group of important shrubs, annuals, biennials, perennials and subshrubs, ranging from tree-like succulents to structural clumps for the border. The latter spurges, evergreen and deciduous, grow in a wide range of conditions, from shade to sun, and tend to be quite sturdy, many leaning at 45° if not standing upright. Many of the evergreens actually benefit from being cut back to produce vigorous new spring growth. For example *E. characias* yields stems covered in small, stiff, outward pointing leaves and yellow-green flowers. A big clump makes a bold, striking feature. *E. griffithii* 'Fireglow', deciduous, is about half as high and

produces early summer orange-red terminal bracts. It spreads to form a large colony. And *E. schillingii*, a recent find in Nepal by plant hunter Tony Schilling, flowers in late summer and has yellow bracts.

CONDITIONS

Aspect	Depending on your choice of plant, spurges like full sun or light shade.
Soil	This too can vary from light, fast-draining soil to damp, moist ground, rich with leaf mould.

GROWING METHOD

Propagation	Sow the seed when ripe, or the following spring. Alternatively divide perennials in the spring, or take spring cuttings.
Feeding	Spurges requiring rich soil can be given a scattering of complete plant food and mulched in spring. Spurges requiring fast-draining ground need only be fed.
Problems	Aphids can be a problem in a bad year; spray at the first sign of an attack.

FLOWERING

Season	Flowers appear in spring or summer.
Cutting	While the stem structure of most spurges makes them theoretically good as cut-flowers, note that the milky sap can badly irritate the skin; if any part of the plant is ingested, severe discomfort results. Wear gloves and goggles.

AFTER FLOWERING

Requirements	Cut back the brownish or lacklustre stems in the autumn to promote fresh new growth.

EUPHORBIA AT A GLANCE

A genus of some 2,000 species. The border kind tend to be grown for their structure. Frost tender to hardy −18°C (0°F).

		RECOMMENDED VARIETIES
JAN	/	
FEB	/	*Euphorbia amygdaloides* var. *robbiae*
MAR	divide	
APR	transplant	*E. characias*
MAY	flowering	*E. characias wulfenii*
JUN	flowering	*E. griffithii* 'Dixter'
JULY	flowering	*E. myrsinites*
AUG	flowering	*E. palustris*
SEPT	flowering	*E. polychroma*
OCT	sow	
NOV	/	
DEC	/	

GERANIUM
Cranesbill

THE FOLIAGE *on this clump-forming, North American* Geranium macrorrhizum *is as attractive as the lovely pink white or pink flowers. The leaves are scented and quickly form a dense carpet.*

GERANIUM PRATENSE *with its deep violet flowers that bloom over a long period.*

FEATURES

HERBACEOUS

EVERGREEN

There are a great many perennial species of the true, hardy geranium, and many are reliable, long-flowering plants. Most cranesbill geraniums (not to be confused with tender, pot-plant pelargoniums) are easy to grow, and are ideal in perennial borders, as edging plants, or as an infill between shrubs. Some species self-sow freely but unwanted seedlings are easily removed. Cranesbills range from about 15cm–1m (6-39in) tall. Most have attractive, deeply divided leaves, and the flowers cover a range of shades, mostly in violet, blue, pink, rose and cerise. Species worth seeking out include *G. endressii* and its cultivars, especially 'Wargrave Pink', *G. pratense*, *G. psilostemon*, *G. himalayense* and *G. sanguineum*. A variety of *G. sanguineum*, 'Lancastriense', is a dwarf-growing type that can be used as groundcover.

GERANIUM AT A GLANCE

A genus of some 300 annuals, biennials, and perennials grown for their big flowering clumps. Most hardy to –15°C (5°F).

JAN	/	
FEB	sow	**RECOMMENDED VARIETIES**
MAR	sow	*Geranium himalayense* 'Gravetye'
APR	divide	'Johnson's Blue'
MAY	transplant	*G. x oxonianum* 'Wargrave Pink'
JUN	flowering	*G. palmatum*
JULY	flowering	*G. pratense* 'Mrs Kendall Clark'
AUG	flowering	*G. psilostemon*
SEPT	flowering	
OCT	sow	
NOV	/	
DEC	/	

CONDITIONS

Aspect Most like sun; others prefer shade.
Site Needs open, well-drained soil, but it need not be rich. Very acid ground should be limed before planting; use a soil-testing kit to ascertain the quantity required.

GROWING METHOD

Propagation Most cranesbills are easily grown from seed sown in the autumn, but note that the results will be variable. They can also be grown from cuttings taken in the growing season. Established clumps can be lifted and divided in the spring. The exact spacing depends on the variety, but it is usually within the range of 20–40cm (8–16in). Established plants tolerate dry conditions and rarely need watering, except in prolonged droughts.
Feeding Apply a little complete plant food as growth starts in the spring.
Problems No specific pest or disease problems are known for these plants.

FLOWERING

Season Cranesbills flower through the spring, into late summer.
Cutting Flowers do not cut well.

AFTER FLOWERING

Requirements Remove spent flower stems unless you want the plants to seed. Some pruning may be needed through the growing season if growth becomes much too rampant. Prune to maintain shape.

GEUM CHILOENSE

Avens

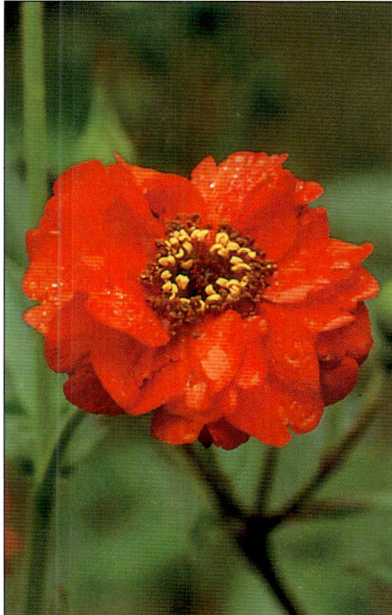

THE BRIGHT RED *double geum 'Mrs J Bradshaw', a justifiably popular perennial.*

LIKE MOST PERENNIALS, *geums look best when planted together in large numbers. Here a mass of deep red flowers looks wonderful against a background of green foliage.*

FEATURES

HERBACEOUS

Although there are many species of geum, the two most commonly grown are cultivars. 'Lady Stratheden' has double yellow flowers, and 'Mrs J Bradshaw' bright scarlet double flowers. Flowers appear on stems 30–50cm (12–20in) high that emerge from large rosettes of slightly hairy, lobed compound leaves. Foliage is generally evergreen, but may be herbaceous in some areas. Geums can be planted as accent plants, preferably in groups, in the wild garden or near the front of a mixed border. While flowers are not very suitable for cutting, they give a long, vibrant display in the garden if they are regularly deadheaded.

GEUM AT A GLANCE

Brightly coloured perennial, essential for the spring border, with plenty of attractive cultivars. All hardy to –18ºC (0ºF).

		RECOMMENDED VARIETIES
JAN	/	'Borisii'
FEB	sow	'Fire Opal'
MAR	divide	'Lady Stratheden'
APR	transplant	G. montanum
MAY	flowering	'Mrs J Bradshaw'
JUN	flowering	G. rivale
JULY	/	G. urbanum
AUG	/	
SEPT	/	
OCT	divide	
NOV	/	
DEC	/	

CONDITIONS

Aspect   Prefers full sun, but it can also be grown successfully in dappled shade.

Site   Needs well-drained soil. Plants will benefit from the addition of plenty of decayed manure or compost before planting.

GROWING METHOD

Propagation   Clumps can be divided in the spring or autumn. Cut back foliage to reduce moisture loss while divisions re-establish. Also grows from seed sown in spring, but plants may not be true to type. Plant about 25–30cm (10–12in) apart. Since most popular varieties tend to be short lived, propagate often for a regular supply.

Feeding   Apply complete plant food in early spring and again in mid-summer.

Problems   No particular problems are known.

FLOWERING

Season   There is a long flowering display through late spring and mid-summer. Young vigorous plants will keep going to the autumn.

Cutting   Regular cutting (or deadheading) is essential to prolong the display.

AFTER FLOWERING

Requirements   None, apart from the removal of spent flower stems and any dead foliage which may accumulate under the rosette.

GUNNERA MANICATA
Gunnera

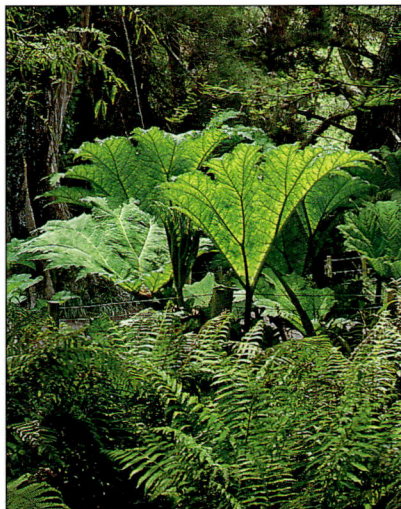

THE HUGE, *theatrical, eye-catching leaves of* Gunnera manicata.

DAMP GROUND *at the bottom of this steep bank allows the clump of gunnera to thrive in its favourite conditions. The lovely pink-flowering shrub beside it is a hawthorn (*Crataegus *species).*

FEATURES

HERBACEOUS

This is not a plant for small gardens. Growing to 2.5m (8½ft) high, clumps grow 3–4m (10–13ft) wide. The huge rhubarb-like leaves can be well over 1m (42in) in diameter, and are supported by long, stout, hairy stems. This is a magnificent feature plant from Africa, Australasia, and S. America. It needs a damp or wet garden area, beside a pond or stream, or to the edge of a lawn. In summer it produces a dramatic tall spike of greenish flowers, often completely concealed by the foliage, but this plant is grown for the impact of its giant, architectural foliage. It is herbaceous, dying right back to the ground in winter. This is not a difficult plant to grow in the right conditions, but it must be carefully sited. It needs space to grow, and gardeners need space to stand back and admire it.

GUNNERA AT A GLANCE

One of the largest, most spectacular perennials, producing huge, often lobed, leaves. Spectacular flower spike. Hardy to –10° (5°F).

		RECOMMENDED VARIETIES
JAN	/	
FEB	/	*Gunnera arenaria*
MAR	/	*G. flavida* (groundcover)
APR	transplant	*G. hamiltonii*
MAY	transplant	*G. magellanica* (ground-
JUN	/	cover)
JULY	flowering	*G. manicata*
AUG	/	*G. prorepens*
SEPT	sow	*G. tinctoria*
OCT	/	
NOV	/	
DEC	/	

CONDITIONS

Aspect   Grows both in semi-shade and sun in cool, damp areas.

Site   Likes a rich, moist soil. Dig plenty of organic matter into the ground before planting, and mulch crowns heavily with decayed compost or manure for protection.

GROWING METHOD

Propagation   Divide small clumps in the spring, replanting them no less than 2m (6½ft) apart. Cuttings can be taken from new growth, too. Pot them up and nurture them until they are well rooted. Plants can be raised from seed, but this is slow and difficult. Keep moist throughout spring and summer.

Feeding   Apply pelleted poultry manure as new growth commences in the early spring to give a boost. Add a fresh mulch of rotted manure at the same time.

Problems   No specific pest or disease problems are known for gunnera.

FLOWERING

Season   Heavy spikes of greenish flowers are produced in early summer.

Fruits   The inflorescence is followed by fleshy red-green fruits, which can be ornamental.

AFTER FLOWERING

Requirements   As the weather becomes cold in the autumn and leaves begin to brown, cut off the foliage and cover the crown of the plant with a thick layer of straw. Use a large leaf as a hat to keep it dry.

GYPSOPHILA PANICULATA

Baby's breath

THE WONDERFUL, MASSED DISPLAY OF Gypsophila paniculata 'Pink Star' in full bloom. The rippling, airy mound of flowers justifiably led to its common name, baby's breath. It makes a stunning sight in its native habitats, spreading across the sandy steppes of the Far East and eastern Europe.

FEATURES

HERBACEOUS

Baby's breath is an eye-catching border perennial that grows to 1.2m (4ft) high, and produces a summer flower display that looks like a puffy aerial cloud. The flowers appear in mid- and late summer, and are white on the species, though there are gently coloured cultivars. 'Compacta Plena' is soft pink, 'Flamingo' is lilac-pink, and 'Rosenschleier' pale pink. The latter is also quite short, at 30cm (1ft) high, and is worth repeat planting in a long border. 'Bristol Fairy' has the advantage of large white flowers, 1.5cm (½in) across, but it is not as vigorous as the rest and

is relatively short lived, needing to be propagated every few years. *G. paniculata* mixes well with contrasting, vertical plants.

CONDITIONS

Aspect Full sun is required for it to thrive.
Site Free-draining soil is essential since the plant's native habitat is sandy steppes and stony sites in eastern Europe, central Asia and China.

GROWING METHOD

Propagation Sow seed in a cold frame in spring, or in pots in a gently heated greenhouse in winter. Species can be propagated by root cuttings, again in late winter. Though adult plants tolerate some dryness, the young plants must not be allowed to dry out. Water regularly in the growing season. Plant out in its final position since it dislikes disturbance.
Feeding A scattering of complete plant food in the spring.
Problems Generally problem free.

FLOWERING

Season The one flowering period is mid- and late summer; an unmissable sight.
Cutting Makes excellent cut flowers, the light sprays of white to pink flowers considerably add to any arrangement, formal or flowery.

AFTER FLOWERING

Requirements Cut back to ground level in the autumn.

GYPSOPHILA AT A GLANCE

A striking, tallish herbaceous perennial giving an impactful, flowery mid-summer display. Hardy to −18° (0°F).

		COMPANION PLANTS
JAN	/	
FEB	/	*Agapanthus africanus*
MAR	sow	*Geranium himalayense*
APR	transplant	*Iris* 'Magic Man'
MAY	/	*Osteospermum* 'Whirligig'
JUN	/	*Salvia cacaliifolia*
JULY	flowering	*Silene coeli-rosa*
AUG	flowering	*Solanum crispum*
SEPT	/	
OCT	/	
NOV	/	
DEC	/	

HELENIUM AUTUMNALE
Sneezeweed

STILL ONE OF THE BEST and most popular cultivars of sneeze-weed, 'Moerheim Beauty' has been a favourite since the 1930s.

ORANGE AND TAWNY COLOURS are a feature of sneezeweed, a reliable perennial that brightens the autumn garden.

FEATURES

HERBACEOUS

As its Latin name suggests, this herbaceous perennial flowers from late summer to mid-autumn. The straight species has bright golden, daisy-like flowers with dark centres, but many of the most popular cultivars have flowers in rich tones of orange-red or copper-red. 'Butterpat', 'Moerheim Beauty' and 'Waldtraut' are among the most popular varieties. Sneezeweed can grow 1–1.5m (39–60in) or more high, eventually forming large clumps over 50cm (20in) across. Flowers cut well, but the plant is probably more valuable for its contribution to the autumn garden. Place at the back of a perennial border or among shrubs. Easy to grow.

HELENIUM AT A GLANCE

A group of annuals, biennials and perennials. Grown for their prolific, bright flowering display. Hardy to –15°C (5°F).

JAN	/	
FEB	sow	
MAR	sow	
APR	transplant	
MAY	transplant	
JUN	/	
JULY	flowering	
AUG	flowering	
SEPT	flowering	
OCT	/	
NOV	/	
DEC	/	

RECOMMENDED VARIETIES

'Butterpat'

'Chipperfield Orange'

'Crimson Beauty'

'Moerheim Beauty'

'Rotgold'

'The Bishop'

CONDITIONS

Aspect Needs to be grown in full sun right through the day. Avoid shade.

Site Needs a moisture-retentive soil heavily enriched with organic matter. It will not thrive in dry soil. Mulch around clumps to help keep soil moist.

GROWING METHOD

Propagation Established clumps can be lifted and divided about every three years. Discard the oldest central sections and replant the divisions about 30cm (12in) apart in spring or autumn. Give new young plants a regular watering right through the growing season.

Feeding Apply complete plant food as new growth commences in spring.

Problems Sneezeweed is generally free from problems, although slugs and snails can damage newly emerging growth in damp weather.

FLOWERING

Season The flowering season starts in mid-summer and continues into the autumn.

Cutting Flowers cut well for indoor decoration.

AFTER FLOWERING

Requirements Spent flower stems should be removed. As the plant dies down, cut off and remove dead foliage. It can be chopped and left on the ground as a mulch. With flowers blooming into the autumn, the foliage remains in good condition until attacked by frost.

HELLEBORUS
Lenten rose

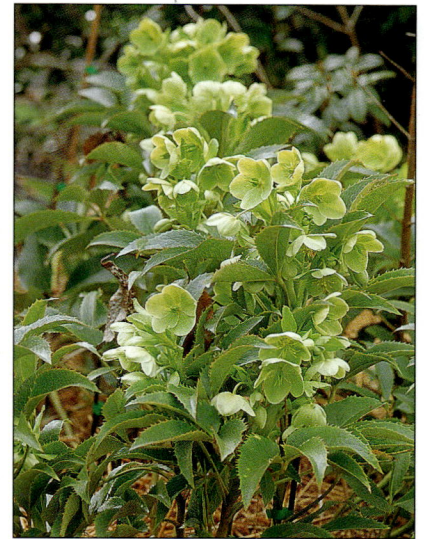

PRETTY SHADINGS *of colour are shown on the Lenten rose. Seedlings often produce unexpected colours, which can be maintained if the plants are then propagated by division.*

NATIVE *to Corsica and Sardinia, this is the green-flowered* Helleborus argutifolius.

FEATURES

SUMMER AUTUMN WINTER SPRING
EVERGREEN

Various species of hellebores are known as the Christmas or Lenten rose because of their flowering times – mid-winter or early spring. *H. niger*, which has pure white flowers with green centres, can be tricky to grow to perfection; *H. argutifolius (*syn. *H. corsicus)* and *H. orientalis* are more resilient. *H. argutifolius* has lovely lime-green flowers and spiny-toothed leaf margins, while *H. orientalis* is more variable and may have white, green, pink or mottled flowers. Cultivars include a deep crimson variety. These perennials are mostly evergreen and are best planted under deciduous trees where they can remain undisturbed. Some are fairly short lived, but they tend to self-seed freely so that numbers readily increase, creating an impressive sight.

HELLEBORUS AT A GLANCE

A free-spreading, attractively flowering perennial in a wide range of colours. Excellent in woodland. Hardy to –5/15ºC (23/º5F).

		RECOMMENDED VARIETIES
JAN	flowering	*Helleborus argutifolius* (syn.
FEB	flowering	*H. corsicus*)
MAR	flowering	*H. foetidus*
APR	divide	*H. lividus*
MAY	transplant	*H. niger*
JUN	/	*H.* x *nigercors*
JULY	/	*H. orientalis* Cultivars
AUG	/	*H.* x *sternii* Blackthorn
SEPT	/	Group
OCT	/	*H. viridis*
NOV	/	
DEC	/	

CONDITIONS

Aspect   Prefers dappled sunlight under trees, or in other partially shaded spots.
Site   Soil must be well enriched with organic matter, and able to retain moisture. Excellent in winter containers.

GROWING METHOD

Propagation   Divide clumps in the spring or summer, straight after flowering, replanting the divisions about 20–30cm (8–12in) apart. Seed can be sown when ripe, but seedlings will take about three years to flower. Seedlings often produce interesting shades. Recently planted hellebores need plenty of water in prolonged, dry spells in spring and summer.
Feeding   Apply a little complete plant food in the spring. Mulch each spring with manure or compost to aid moisture retention.
Problems   Leaf blotch can disfigure and weaken plants. Spray with a fungicide. Beware aphids, particularly after flowering. Slugs attack the flowers and foliage.

FLOWERING

Season   From mid-winter to early spring.
Cutting   Lenten roses provide attractive cut flowers at the time of year when supply is rather short.

AFTER FLOWERING

Requirements   Prune off the dead flower stems and any dead leaves. Do not disturb.

HEMEROCALLIS
Daylily

MAHOGANY RED is one of the many strong colours available in the huge range of daylily cultivars now available from specialist growers.

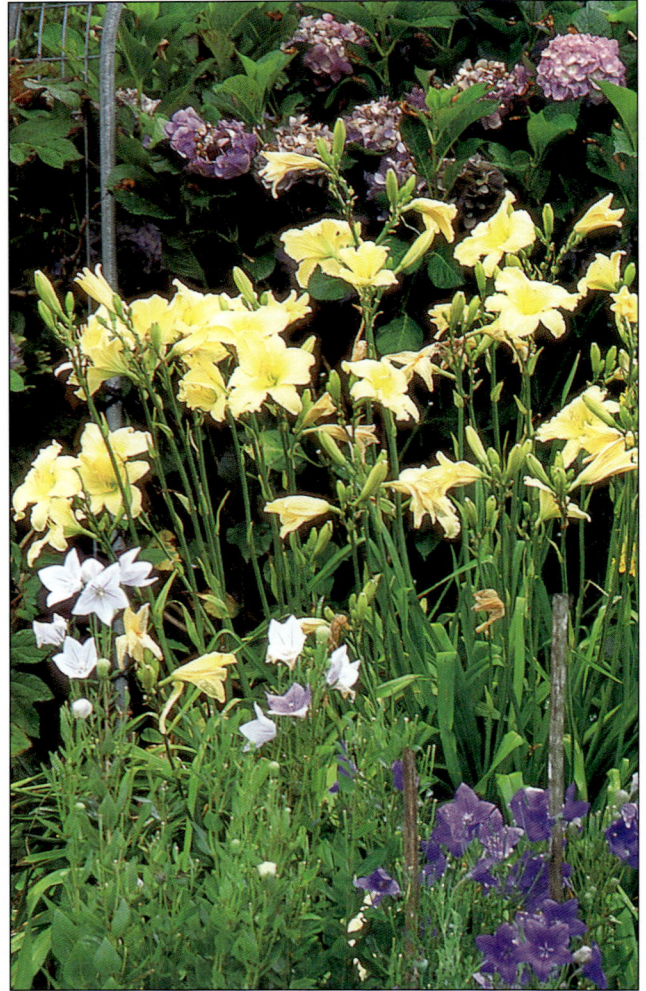

THE MASS PLANTING of this creamy yellow daylily increases its impact. Blooms will appear one after the other for many weeks.

FEATURES

HERBACEOUS

EVERGREEN

Easily grown in a wide range of conditions, the daylily is a trouble-free plant with single or double flowers. As its name suggests, individual flowers last only one day, but they are produced over a long period. They come in a wide range of colours, the main ones being shades of yellow, orange, red, magenta and purple. There is an enormous number of exciting, attractive hybrids available from specialist growers. The clumps of grassy foliage may be from 25cm–1m (10–39in) high; some are evergreen while others die down in winter.

While straight species are not as readily available as the hybrids, they are important in hybridising new varieties and several species are worth seeking out. They include *H. altissima* from China, which has pale yellow fragrant flowers on stems 1.5m (5ft) or so high, and *H. lilio-asphodelus*, which has pale yellow fragrant flowers above leaves 55cm (22in) high.

Categories Daylilies have been divided into five categories which list them according to flower type. The divisions are circular, double, spider-shaped, star-shaped and triangular. Most are single; hot weather can produce extra petals and stamens.

Dwarf forms The number of dwarf forms available is steadily increasing and they may be better suited to today's smaller gardens. Those with a reliable reflowering habit can also be successfully grown in pots. Use a good quality potting mix and crowd three plants into a 20cm (8in) pot for good effect. 'Little Grapette', 'Little Gypsy Vagabond', 'Penny's Worth', and 'Stella d'Oro' are good ones to try, all growing about 30 x 45cm (12 x 18in).

Uses Mass plantings of dwarf or tall forms create the best effect. Daylilies are not plants that should be dotted about in the garden. Use large numbers of either the one variety or use varieties of similar colour; it is clearly preferable to planting a mixture of types or colours. In a mixed border they give a very pleasing effect as the foliage is very full.

'BURNING DAYLIGHT', one of the top daylilies, blooms prolifically in sun or semi-shade.

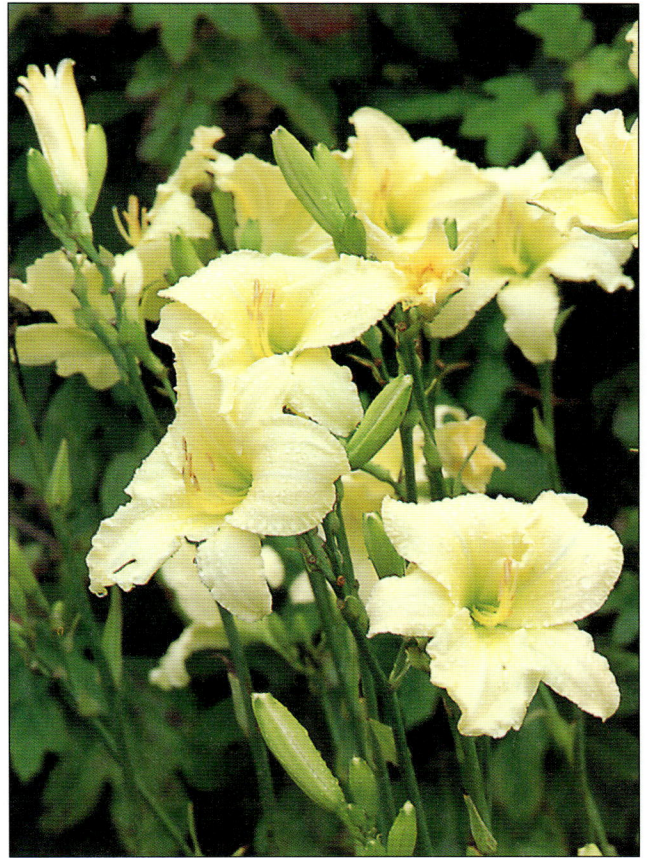

MANY OF the finest daylily cultivars are in creamy yellow or orange tones, not surprisingly as these are the colours of many of the species.

CONDITIONS

Aspect Grows best in full sun but tolerates semi-shade. Can be mass planted on banks or sloping ground as the roots are very efficient soil binders.

Site Grows in any type of soil, wet or dry, but to get maximum growth from the newer hybrids the soil should be enriched with manure or compost before planting.

HEMEROCALLIS AT A GLANCE

A genus of semi-, evergreen, and herbaceous perennials; 30,000 cultivars that give a long summer show. Hardy to −15°C (5°F).

		RECOMMENDED VARIETIES
JAN	/	
FEB	sow	'Burning Daylight'
MAR	sow	'Cartwheels'
APR	transplant	'Golden Chimes'
MAY	transplant	'Neyron Rose'
JUN	flowering	'Pink Damask'
JULY	flowering	'Red Precious'
AUG	flowering	'Stafford'
SEPT	flowering	'Whichford'
OCT	divide	'Zara'
NOV	/	
DEC	/	

GROWING METHOD

Propagation Divide established clumps in spring or autumn. Cut back foliage before or straight after division. Spacing may be from 15–30cm (6–12in), depending on variety. New plants need regular watering to establish. Once established, plants are very drought tolerant, but better sized blooms can be expected if deep waterings are given every week or two.

Feeding Grows without supplementary fertiliser, but an application of complete plant food in early spring encourages stronger, more vigorous growth.

Problems Daylilies growing in very soggy ground tend to survive quite well but produce few flowers. Otherwise no problems.

FLOWERING

Season Depending on variety, plants may be in bloom any time from late spring until autumn. Most flowers only last one day.

Cutting Single flowers can be cut for the vase. Attractive and well worth using.

AFTER FLOWERING

Requirements Cut off any spent flower stems. Herbaceous types that die down in the autumn can have their foliage cut back too.

HEUCHERA SANGUINEA
Coral flower

DAINTY LITTLE PINK FLOWERS are massed above the attractive foliage, making the North American coral flower an excellent choice for the front of a border or a garden bed. Here they are planted to provide an excellent foil for the abundant blooms of white roses behind.

FEATURES

SUMMER AUTUMN WINTER SPRING
EVERGREEN

This perennial forms a low rosette of lobed leaves which make a neat plant for edging, or mass planting at the front of the border. The foliage is evergreen. Established plantings produce a striking display of blooms. The flower stems, which stand above the foliage, are from 30–45cm (12–18in) high. The species has red flowers, cultivars are available with pink, white or deeper crimson blooms. Note the superb foliage varieties ('Palace Purple' – chocolate coloured, 'Pewter Moon' – grey, and 'Snow Storm' – white flecked). New American ones include 'Pewter Veil'.

HEUCHERA AT A GLANCE

H. sanguinea is a red-flowering, summer perennial forming low, wide clumps, 15 x 30cm (6 x 12in). Hardy to –15°C (5°F).

		RECOMMENDED PLANTS
JAN	/	*Heuchera americana*
FEB	sow	'Chocolate Ruffles'
MAR	sow	*H. cylindrica*
APR	divide	'Green Ivory'
MAY	transplant	'Helen Dillon'
JUN	flowering	'Persian Carpet'
JULY	flowering	'Pewter Moon'
AUG	flowering	'Rachel'
SEPT	/	'Red Spangles'
OCT	divide	'Scintillation'
NOV	/	
DEC	/	

CONDITIONS

Aspect Prefers full sun but tolerates light shade.
Site Needs very well-drained, open-textured soil. Permanently wet soil will kill this plant.

GROWING METHOD

Propagation Clumps can be divided in the spring or in the autumn, but do ensure that each division has its own set of healthy roots. It can also be grown from seed sown in the spring; cuttings will also root quite freely. Plant at approximately 20–25cm (8–10in) intervals for a good effect.

Feeding Apply a complete plant food when growth commences in the spring.

Problems Vine weevil grubs may devour roots and stems. Destroy the infected clump, and use severed shoots as cuttings.

FLOWERING

Season It flowers well through most of the summer, with a few spikes hanging on until the early autumn.

Cutting Flowers do not last well as cut blooms.

AFTER FLOWERING

Requirements Promptly remove any spent flower stems once they begin to look tatty and untidy. Apart from the removal of any dead leaves, this is all that is necessary.

HOSTA
Plantain lily

LEAVES PATTERNED VARIOUSLY in lime-green and blue make this Hosta *'Frances Williams' an outstanding garden feature. Here it lights up a dull area under a tree, the little available light being reflected outwards by the lime-green. In shady areas where few flowers bloom, it is a real bonus.*

FEATURES

HERBACEOUS

Also known as the plantain lily, this herbaceous perennial is grown for its attractive, decorative foliage. It is long lived, and foliage may be tiny or up to 45cm (18in) wide and 90cm (36in) high. There are hundreds of cultivars with leaves that may be light or dark green, chartreuse or yellow, grey-green or blue. Many are variegated. Leaf texture also varies: it can be smooth or shiny, matt or powdery, puckered or corrugated. Hostas are excellent at forming big, bold clumps that keep down the weeds, but until they emerge in late spring some weeding will be necessary; they also benefit from heavy mulching. Hostas look best mass planted near water features, or when allowed to multiply in shady areas under trees.

Variegations
Cultivars with cream, white or yellow variegations will brighten a shady part of the garden, and as long as the tree or shrub canopy is high enough to let sufficient light reach the hostas, they will maintain their variegation. Likewise plants with sharp chartreuse or acid-lime coloured foliage can be used to give a lift to shady areas. Types can be mixed to create a wealth of different effects.

Flowers
The bell-shape flowers, mostly in mauve shades, appear in summer, being held high above the foliage. Some species such as *H. plantaginea* and its cultivar 'Grandiflora' produce pure white, lightly fragrant flowers. However, few plant hostas just for the flowers; the leaves alone are good enough.

HOSTA AT A GLANCE

A mainly clump-forming perennial from the Far East. Grow in pots or the garden for the foliage. Hardy to –18°C (0°F).

		RECOMMENDED VARIETIES
JAN	/	
FEB	/	'Aureomarginata'
MAR	sow	'Blue Angel'
APR	divide	'Francee'
MAY	transplant	'Frances Williams'
JUN	flowering	'Golden Tiara'
JULY	flowering	'Love Pat'
AUG	divide	*H. lancifolia*
SEPT	flowering	'Shade Fanfare'
OCT	/	'Wide Brim'
NOV	/	
DEC	/	

STRONGLY PUCKERED LEAVES in a bluish colour and white flowers are characteristic of Hosta sieboldiana *'Elegans'.*

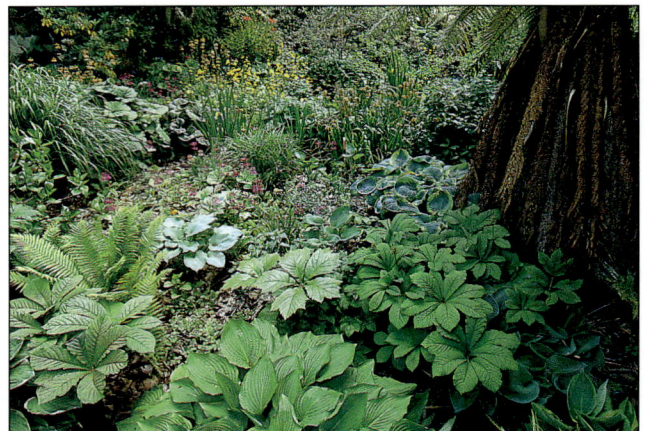

PURE WHITE FLOWERS appear on some species of hosta such as Hosta plantaginea *and some of its cultivars.*

HOSTAS, RODGERSIAS and ferns revel in the light shade and constant damp soil prevalent in woodlands.

Companions Since hostas do not come into leaf early in spring, the early-flowering bulbs, such as snowdrops and snowflakes, or early perennials, such as corydalis, can be planted among them. They make a bright, successful show.

CONDITIONS

Aspect Most hostas grow in full sun if well watered. They thrive in shade or dappled light. Blue-leaved forms can be the hardest of all to place because they turn green with either too much sun, or too heavy shade. Yellow or gold forms are best with direct sun in the early morning, or late in the afternoon.

Site Needs rich, moisture-retentive soil. Large amounts of decayed manure or compost should be dug into the ground well before planting. Mulch plants after planting. Superb in tubs, getting bigger and better each year.

GROWING METHOD

Propagation Divide the fleshy underground rhizomes in early spring. Most hostas are best divided every four to five years. Plant the dwarf cultivars

15cm (6in) apart, the larger ones at intervals of 90cm (36in). Several species can be raised from seed, though they may not be true to type.

Feeding Apply pelletted poultry manure in the spring.

Problems Slugs and snails can be a major problem. Pick off snails, and avoid watering in the evening. Place slug pellets or sharp sand around the leaves.

FLOWERING

Season Flowers are produced in the summer. The colour range varies from white to purple.

Cutting Hosta provides cut flowers; the foliage is also attractive.

AFTER FLOWERING

Requirements Cut off any spent flower stems in spring. Continue watering the plants until the foliage begins to die down, and then tidy up the clumps which can look rather unsightly. Mulch the area with supplies of compost or manure. Some hostas (*sieboldiana*) produce good autumn tints. The seedheads can be left on for winter decoration.

KNIPHOFIA
Red hot poker

*FLAME COLOURED pokers and soft pur-
ple perovskia both tolerate dry conditions.*

*THE COLOURS in this generous planting of red hot pokers reflect both the yellow achillea behind
and the red plants in the foreground. The abundant grassy foliage provides a valuable contrast.*

FEATURES

EVERGREEN

These evergreen perennials, also known as
torch lilies, make great feature plants with
their bright flower spikes in cream, orange,
red, yellow and many shadings of these
colours. Flower stems stand high above the
grassy foliage, which may be anywhere from
60cm–2m (24in–6½ft) high. Even out of
flower the distinctive foliage makes red hot
poker a good accent plant. Since clumps
should remain undisturbed for many years,
plant in their final position.

CONDITIONS

Aspect   Needs full sun all day. A valuable plant
because it tolerates a wide range of exposed
windy or coastal areas.

KNIPHOFIA AT A GLANCE

A genus of some 70 species of evergreen and deciduous perennials, grown for their flowering spires. Hardy to –15°C (5°F).

		RECOMMENDED VARIETIES
JAN	/	
FEB	/	'Bees Sunset'
MAR	sow	'Brimstone'
APR	divide	'Buttercup'
MAY	transplant	*K. caulescens*
JUN	flowering	'Little Maid'
JULY	flowering	'Royal Standard'
AUG	flowering	'Samuel's Sensation'
SEPT	flowering	'Sunningdale Yellow'
OCT	flowering	*K. triangularis*
NOV	/	
DEC	/	

Site   Needs well-drained soil. Although it tolerates
poorer soils, especially sandy ones, you will get
better results if the soil is enriched with
manure or compost.

GROWING METHOD

Propagation   Well-established clumps can be divided in late
spring. Foliage on new divisions must be
reduced by half to allow successful root
regrowth to take place. The smaller-growing
forms can be planted at 50cm (20in) spacings,
but the large growers may need up to 76cm
(30in) or more. Needs regular watering to
establish in prolonged dry spells, after which it
is very drought tolerant.

Feeding   Grows without supplementary fertiliser, but
complete plant food applied in the spring
should noticeably increase the quantity and
quality of the flowers.

Problems   No specific problems are known.

FLOWERING

Season   Flowering times can vary slightly with species
and cultivar. Generally, red hot pokers flower
in late summer and early autumn.

Cutting   The flowers last well when cut if the stems are
scalded for approximately 10 seconds. They
make an invaluable tall, stiff background for a
display of smaller, flowery cuttings.

AFTER FLOWERING

Requirements   Spent flower stalks should be promptly cut off.
Any dead leaves should be pulled away to give
the clump a clean look. Protect the crown with
straw or leaves in cold areas.

LEUCANTHEMUM
Shasta daisy

LONG-STEMMED shasta daisies are an ideal component of flower arrangements.

A CONTINUOUS PLANTING of shasta daisies fills this awkward narrow space between a path and a low brick wall. The cheerful white flowers appear throughout the summer.

FEATURES

SUMMER AUTUMN WINTER SPRING

HERBACEOUS

Leucanthemum x *superbum* (Shasta daisy) looks wonderful when planted in a mixed border where the large white flowers mix with more brightly coloured flowers. Despite being easy to grow and multiplying rapidly, the daisies do not become a menace. Flower stalks can grow 60–90cm (24–36in) high, while the dark green leaves are only 10–15cm (4–6in) high. Shasta daisies make striking cut flowers, livening up any arrangement. There are a number of named cultivars, some such as 'Esther Read', 'Wirral Supreme' and 'Cobham Gold' with double flowers. (Despite its name, the flowers on 'Cobham Gold' are cream, not gold.) 'Everest' is probably the largest of the single cultivars, though it is rarely available.

LEUCANTHEMUM AT A GLANCE

L. x *superbum* is a vigorous, clump-forming perennial with many attractive cultivars mainly in white. Hardy to –5°C (5°F).

JAN	/	
FEB	/	
MAR	divide	
APR	transplant	
MAY	transplant	
JUN	flowering	
JULY	flowering	
AUG	flowering	
SEPT	flowering	
OCT	divide	
NOV	/	
DEC	/	

RECOMMENDED VARIETIES

Leucanthemum x *superbum*
'Aglaia'
'Alaska'
'Bishopstone'
'Cobham Gold'
'Horace Read'
'Phyllis Smith'
'Snowcap'

CONDITIONS

Aspect Prefers full sun all day and wind protection.
Site The soil should be well drained, and improved by the addition of decayed compost or manure.

GROWING METHOD

Propagation Divide the clumps in early spring or late summer, replanting only the younger, vigorous, outer growths, each with its own set of roots and shoots. Plant the divisions approximately 25cm (10in) apart. Cuttings of young, short shoots can also be taken in early spring.

Feeding Apply complete plant food as growth begins in spring. Liquid fertiliser applied in late spring should help produce better blooms.

Problems The main problems are aphids, slugs, earwigs, and chrysanthemum eelworm. The first can be tackled with a proprietary spray, and the second and third by traps (saucers filled with beer, and inverted flower pots filled with straw placed on bamboo canes). In the case of eelworm, evident from browning–blackening, drying foliage from the base up, the whole plant must be destroyed.

FLOWERING

Season Flowering is all summer long.
Cutting Cut flowers regularly for indoor decoration, which will also prolong the garden display.

AFTER FLOWERING

Requirements Cut back spent flower stems to the ground.

LIGULARIA
Ligularia

A MARVELLOUS ligularia display. Spikes of bright yellow, eye-catching flowers. No matter what size your border, there is a suitable ligularia. They vary from the medium to tall, at 1.8m (6ft). Big groupings invariably succeed much better than a few individual flowers.

FEATURES

HERBACEOUS

Ligularia, with its bright yellow daisies, has four key advantages. It mainly flowers in mid- and late summer, tolerates dappled shade making it invaluable for the border, and often has interesting, well-displayed foliage. It can be shaped like a kidney, a five-pointed star, or be oval, held on tallish stems. The fourth advantage is that these are tall plants, adding height to schemes, being from 90cm–1.8m (36in–6ft) tall. They can be used in small groups to punctuate arrangements of smaller plants, or form an impressive massed display. The flowers are yellow or orange. *L. dentata* 'Othello' has purple-tinged leaves with a red underside and 'Desdemona' has brownish-green leaves, similarly coloured beneath. With room for only one, 'The Rocket' offers height, yellow flowers, black stems, and interesting, big toothed foliage.

CONDITIONS

Aspect   Tolerates full sun and some light shade. Also requires shelter from cutting winds.

Site   The soil must be moist – ligularias grow well beside ponds and streams – for a big performance. If the soil begins to dry out to any degree the plants quickly show signs of distress by wilting.

GROWING METHOD

Propagation   Increase the species by sowing seed or division in the spring or autumn. Cultivars can only be raised by division. Make sure that the emerging new growth is well-watered, and never allowed to dry out. Set out from 60cm–1.2m (24in–4ft) apart.

Feeding   Border plants need plenty of well-rotted manure or compost, and a deep mulch to guard against moisture loss.

Problems   Slugs and snails can be a major problem, especially as the leaves emerge. Pick off or treat chemically.

FLOWERING

Season   Generally from late summer into autumn, but some flower in mid-summer, and *L. stenocephala* in early summer.

Cutting   It is not advisable to strip the plants of their impressive flowering stems, especially when you only have room for a few plants.

AFTER FLOWERING

Requirements Cut back to the ground.

LIGULARIA AT A GLANCE

A genus of 150 species of perennials grown for their tall flower spikes and large, architectural foliage. Hardy to –18°C (0°F).

JAN	/	
FEB	sow	
MAR	sow	
APR	transplant	
MAY	transplant	
JUN	/	
JULY	flowering	
AUG	flowering	
SEPT	/	
OCT	divide	
NOV	/	
DEC	/	

RECOMMENDED VARIETIES

Ligularia dentata
L. d. 'Desdemona'
L. d. 'Othello'
'Gregynog Gold'
L. przewalskii
'The Rocket'
L.wilsoniana

LIMONIUM LATIFOLIUM
Sea lavender

THE MOST FAMILIAR annual statice is Limonium sinuatum *'Blue Peter'.*

SEA LAVENDER has broad, slightly fleshy leaves, and flowers for several months. It is equally successful as part of a free-flowing design or, as shown, as a segregated, eye-catching feature.

FEATURES

EVERGREEN

HERBACEOUS

Limonium latifolium (sea lavender) is a perennial type of statice often grown for its tall, finely branched stems of tiny white and pale lavender flowers, which are widely used both in fresh and dried floral arrangements. Flower stems may be over 50cm (20in) high, and the cultivar 'Violetta' has deep violet flowers. The plant forms a basal rosette of broad, rounded, slightly fleshy leaves growing around 25cm (10in) high. Clumps may ultimately spread 45cm (18in) or more wide. This is a good plant for rockeries because it is quite drought tolerant. Sea lavender is native to parts of south-east and central Europe, thriving in dry summers and cold winters.

LIMONIUM AT A GLANCE

L. latifolium is a perennial grown in windy coastal areas for its abundant, late summer flowers. Hardy to −18°C (0°F).

		COMPANION PLANTS
JAN	/	
FEB	/	Eremurus
MAR	divide	Escallonia
APR	transplant	Linum
MAY	/	Kniphofia
JUN	/	Olearia
JULY	/	Perovskia
AUG	flowering	Scabiosa
SEPT	flowering	
OCT	sow	
NOV	/	
DEC	/	

CONDITIONS

Aspect Prefers full sun all day, and tolerates exposed windy or coastal sites.

Site The soil must be very well drained, but need not be rich. In fact, sea lavender tolerates very poor soil.

GROWING METHOD

Propagation Grows from seed sown as soon as it is ripe, when the flowers have dried and turned brown, or from root cuttings taken in spring. New plantings should be spaced about 25–30cm (10–12in) apart. Water regularly to establish new plants, and then give an occasional deep soaking during prolonged dry spring and summer weather.

Feeding Does not need feeding, but a little complete plant food may be applied in early spring, giving a decent boost.

Problems Heavy, poorly drained soils or overwatering may cause the plant to rot and collapse.

FLOWERING

Season Sea lavender flowers in late summer, when its spikelets of lavender flowers with white calyces begin to appear.

Cutting Flowers can be cut for drying when most of the flowers on the stem have fully opened.

AFTER FLOWERING

Requirements Cut off any remaining flower stems when they are past their best.

LIRIOPE MUSCARI
Lilyturf

STRIKING FLOWER SPIKES in deep violet add to the attraction of this variegated form of liriope.

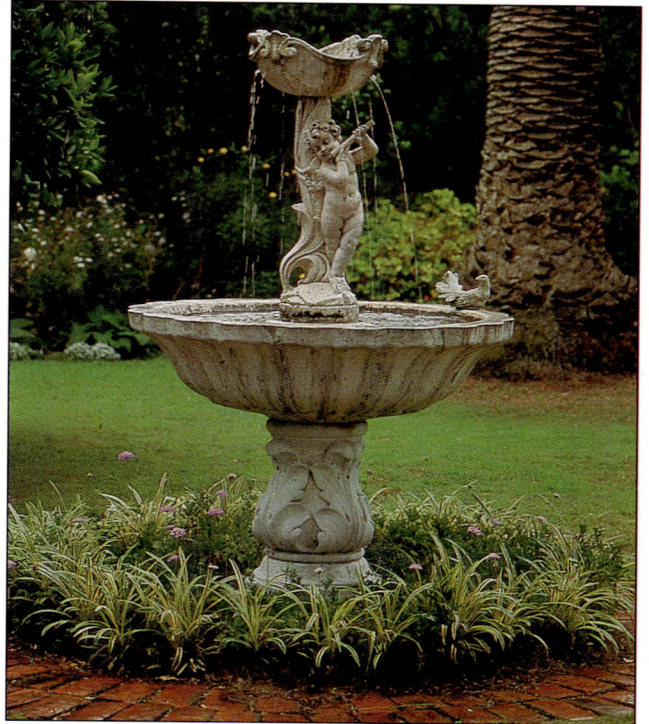

AMONG ITS MANY USES, liriope makes an excellent edging for garden beds. Here it accentuates the circular form of the fountain.

FEATURES

SUMMER AUTUMN WINTER SPRING

HERBACEOUS

This plant, known as lilyturf, is sometimes confused with *Ophiopogon jaburan* which is called white lilyturf. The two are similar but *Ophiopogon* has white flowers. Liriope grows in early summer about 30–35cm (12–14in) high. The species has dark green leaves, but there are variegated forms as well. A spike of deep violet flowers stands well above the leaves. A tough and useful Far Eastern plant for the garden, especially as it flowers in the autumn.

LIRIOPE AT A GLANCE

L. muscari is a stout perennial ideal for difficult places, which also provides good ground cover. Hardy to −18°C (0°F).

JAN	/	
FEB	/	**RECOMMENDED VARIETIES**
MAR	sow	*Liriope muscari* 'Big Blue'
APR	divide	*L. m.* 'Gold Banded'
MAY	transplant	*L. m.* 'Majestic'
JUN	/	*L. m.* 'Monroe White'
JULY	/	
AUG	/	**COMPANION PLANTS**
SEPT	flowering	Dicentra
OCT	flowering	Dryopteris
NOV	flowering	*Euphorbia robbiae*
DEC	/	Polypodium
		Ribes

CONDITIONS

Aspect   Will grow in shade or dappled sunlight, but flowers best in full sun.

Site   Tolerates most soils but acid is preferred; grows best in well-drained soil enriched with plenty of organic matter.

GROWING METHOD

Propagation   The easiest method of increase is to lift and divide the clumps in the spring. Replant the divisions approximately 7.5–10cm (3–4in) apart. Water young plants regularly during prolonged dry spring and summer weather. Plants tolerate drought but prefer some regular water.

Feeding   Apply complete plant food in the spring.

Problems   No specific problems are known.

FLOWERING

Season   The flowering begins in the early autumn, and continues until the end of the season.

Cutting   Lasts quite well in water.

AFTER FLOWERING

Requirements   Cut off spent flowerheads once the flowers have dropped. As growth dies down towards winter, cut it off cleanly.

LOBELIA CARDINALIS
Cardinal flower

THIS LOBELIA is also known as cardinal flower, an apt description as the tall spikes of flowers are the same scarlet as a cardinal's robes.

IN ITS NATURAL HABITAT in North America this lobelia grows on wet meadows and river banks. It thrives on plenty of moisture.

FEATURES

HERBACEOUS

Lobelia to most people is a small edging plant with bright blue flowers. There are, however, about 400 species of lobelia, many of them perennials. This herbaceous species with bright scarlet flowers is also known as the cardinal flower and grows to about 90cm (36in) tall. With its dark green leaves and bright flowers it really stands out and it is sometimes used as a feature plant. It can also be used in a mixed border or mass planted among shrubs as long as the ground retains plenty of moisture.

CONDITIONS

Aspect Grows in full sun or semi-shade.
Site Needs rich and moisture-retentive soil as these plants are not tolerant of drought. A streamside setting is ideal.

GROWING METHOD

Propagation Plants are usually divided every two or three years, in spring. Plant the divisions about 30cm (12in) apart. Lobelia must be kept moist and well watered while it is in active growth, especially during prolonged dry spells in the spring and summer.
Feeding Apply a complete plant food, and a mulch of compost or manure in the spring.
Problems Slugs and snails will attack the flower spikes. Put down slug pellets or beer traps.

FLOWERING

Season There is a long flowering period through the summer and autumn period when the brilliant scarlet blooms appear.
Cutting Flowers are not suitable for cutting.

AFTER FLOWERING

Requirements Cut off spent flower stems. The dark-leaved hybrids ('Cherry Ripe') are not fully hardy and need a thick, protective winter mulch.

LOBELIA AT A GLANCE

L. cardinalis is a clump-forming, short-lived perennial, grown for its striking, vivid red flowers. Hardy to –15°C (5°F).

			RECOMMENDED VARIETIES
JAN	/		*Lobelia* 'Cherry Ripe'
FEB	/		'Dark Crusader'
MAR	sow		'Kompliment Scharlach'
APR	divide		'Queen Victoria'
MAY	transplant		*L. siphilitica*
JUN	/		*L. tupa*
JULY	flowering		
AUG	flowering		
SEPT	flowering		
OCT	/		
NOV	/		
DEC	/		

LUPINUS POLYPHYLLUS
Lupins

RUSSELL LUPINS are noteworthy for their rich colours, including this pinky-red.

LUPINS ARE traditional favourites for perennial borders, where they provide vertical interest. Here they are growing among oriental poppies, campion and grey-leaved germander.

FEATURES

HERBACEOUS

This herbaceous perennial lupin is generally known as the Russell lupin, named after the hybridiser who began developing many fine strains of this plant early this century. It produces tall, densely-packed spires of blooms in a myriad of colours. Growing well over 1m (42in) high, these are plants for a massed display. They flower in early to mid-summer and can look unsightly after flowering; placed at the back of a border the problem is solved. Although they can be cut for indoor use they give much more value in the garden, with several spikes per plant. The only irritation is that plants can be short lived, and should therefore be divided regularly.

LUPINUS AT A GLANCE

L. polyphyllus is an attractive, summer-flowering perennial with striking vertical spires of purple flowers. Hardy to −15°C (5°F).

		RECOMMENDED VARIETIES
JAN	/	
FEB	/	Band of Noble Series
MAR	sow	'Esmerelder'
APR	transplant	'Helen Sharman'
MAY	transplant	'Kayleigh Ann Savage'
JUN	flowering	'Olive Tolley'
JULY	flowering	'Pope John Paul'
AUG	/	'The Page'
SEPT	/	'The Chatelaine'
OCT	sow	
NOV	/	
DEC	/	

CONDITIONS

Aspect Grows in full sun or semi-shade, but it does need wind protection.

Site Soil need not be rich, moderate fertility will suffice, but it must be well drained. Light, slightly sandy, acidic soil is ideal.

GROWING METHOD

Propagation Division of these plants may be difficult. Many strains come true from seed, which should be soaked in warm water before planting in the spring or autumn. Cuttings can be taken from new shoots emerging from the crown in early spring. Set plants approximately 30–40cm (12–16in) apart. Give ample water to young plants to help them establish.

Feeding Needs little fertiliser as lupins fix nitrogen in nodules on their roots. High potash fertiliser may be applied as buds begin to form.

Problems Powdery mildew may be a problem in humid conditions; if necessary spray with a fungicide. Control lupin aphids with an appropriate spray. Virus may cause stunting and discoloration. Destroy affected plants.

FLOWERING

Season Early and mid-summer.

Cutting Flowers may be cut for the vase.

AFTER FLOWERING

Requirements Cut off spent flower stems before they manage to set seed. This will encourage smaller spikes to follow.

LYCHNIS CORONARIA
Rose campion

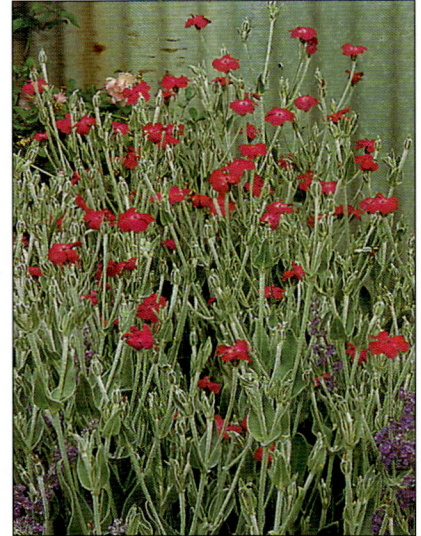

THE DISTINCTIVE ARRANGEMENT of petals on Lychnis chalcedonica *has given rise to its common name, Maltese cross. The bright red flowers show up well against white or blue flowers.*

TRUE CAMPION, Lychnis coronaria, *has abundant, bright cerise flowers.*

FEATURES

HERBACEOUS

Rosettes of soft, silver-grey foliage make *Lychnis coronaria* a very useful plant in the garden, and they contrast with the deep cerise or magenta flowers that appear on stems 30–40cm (12–16in) high. There is also a white flowered form. Easily grown in a sunny, well-drained spot, rose campion tends to be short lived, but it self-seeds prolifically providing a fresh supply. It can be grown as a border plant or as part of a mixed perennial display. *L. flos-jovis* is another species where silvery foliage effectively combines with purple-red blooms. Another popular species of lychnis is the Maltese cross, *L. chalcedonica*, which has mid-green leaves and produces a rounded head of bright scarlet flowers. Pink and white forms, and a double, 'Flore Plena', are also available.

LYCHNIS AT A GLANCE

L. coronaria is a flowery, short-lived purple-red perennial that gives a prolific late summer display. Hardy to –15°C (5°F).

		RECOMMENDED VARIETIES
JAN	/	*Lychnis alpina*
FEB	/	*L. chalcedonica*
MAR	sow	*L. coronaria* Alba Group
APR	division	*L. c.* Atrosanguinea Group
MAY	transplant	*L. flos-cuculi*
JUN	/	*L. viscaria* subsp. 'Splendens Plena'
JULY	flowering	*L. yunnanensis*
AUG	flowering	
SEPT	flowering	
OCT	sow	
NOV	/	
DEC	/	

CONDITIONS

Aspect Grows best in full sun, but it tolerates shade for part of the day.

Site Needs very well-drained soil, but the soil need not be especially rich.

GROWING METHOD

Propagation Tends to self-seed. These plants may show variation from the parent plant. Divide clumps in spring, discard the oldest, lack-lustre sections, and space the new vigorous ones about 20cm (8in) apart. There are some lovely strains to be raised from seed, with mixtures of white, deep violet, carmine, and rose-pink flowers, and a pastel eye.

Feeding Needs little fertiliser. A little complete plant food may be given in early spring.

Problems No pest or disease problems are known, but overwatering or prolonged summer rain in heavy ground may cause rotting.

FLOWERING

Season Flowers in mid- to late summer, but the wait is well worth it with a big showy display that maintains interest in the border at a time when many other plants are flagging.

Cutting Flowers are unsuitable for cutting.

AFTER FLOWERING

Requirements If you do not want plants to self-seed, dead-head with vigilance as the flowers fade. This should also prolong blooming. Completely spent stems should be cut off as low to the ground as possible.

LYSIMACHIA PUNCTATA
Loosestrife

A STRONG, MASSED DISPLAY of loosestrife. Individually unremarkable, a clump makes a splendid feature beside a pond or stream.

FEATURES

EVERGREEN

HERBACEOUS

Loosestrife, which is widely naturalised in Europe and north-east North America, has stalks of bright yellow flowers in summer. It thrives in damp, boggy ground and can easily become invasive. The flowering stems reach 90cm (3ft) high, bearing slightly coarse foliage. Other species offer white flowers on stiff, blue-green stems *(L. ephemerum),* while *L. nummularia* 'Aurea' is a complete contrast. It grows 5cm (2in) high, but spreads indefinitely with evergreen, bright yellow leaves and summer flowers in a matching colour. With room for only one, try *L. clethroides* which has attractive white flowers (90 x 60cm (36 x 24in). The new variegated form *L. p.* 'Alexander' is a great success.

LYSIMACHIA AT A GLANCE

L. punctata is an erect, herbaceous perennial grown for its yellow flowers and ability to colonise damp areas. Hardy to –18ºC (0ºF).

		RECOMMENDED VARIETIES
JAN	/	
FEB	/	*Lysimachia atropurpurea*
MAR	/	*L. ciliata*
APR	divide	*L. clethroides*
MAY	/	*L. minoricensis*
JUN	flowering	*L. nummularia* 'Aurea'
JULY	flowering	*L. thyrsiflora*
AUG	flowering	*L. vulgaris*
SEPT	/	
OCT	divide	
NOV	/	
DEC	/	

CONDITIONS

Aspect   Loosestrife tolerates both full sun and light, dappled shade, but growing in the former gives by far the best results.

Site   Moist ground is essential. Add plenty of organic matter to border plants, and mulch well to guard against moisture loss.

GROWING METHOD

Propagation   Seed can be difficult. The most reliable method is by spring or autumn division.

Feeding   Humus-rich ground produces the best display. Fork plenty of well-rotted manure and compost around the plants in the spring.

Problems   Colonies of slugs and snails can be a major problem, attacking and disfiguring the new, emerging foliage. Either pick off by hand or treat chemically. Plants grown in areas cut by strong winds may need to be staked.

FLOWERING

Season   Flowers appear in summer, timing depending on your chosen variety.

Cutting   They make unremarkable cut flowers, given the enormous competition in summer, but are nonetheless very useful when bulking out large displays with their flowering spires.

AFTER FLOWERING

Requirements   Cut back the old, spent flowering stems down to the ground.

MACLEAYA CORDATA
Plume poppy

THE PLUME POPPY starts inauspiciously, but quickly puts out tall, white summer flowers making it an indispensable feature. It is a key ingredient for the back of the border, where its lobed, olive-green foliage makes a lovely background for smaller plants. The plume poppy does not need staking.

FEATURES

HERBACEOUS

The plume poppy is an essential plant for the back of the border, tall, graceful and showy. Growing 2.5m (8ft) high, it sports long, thin stems with mid- and late summer panicles of pale white flowers. 'Flamingo' has pinkish flowers. The large, lobed foliage is equally attractive. With more room in the border *M. microcarpa* can be grown. It is slightly invasive and has pink flowers, while 'Kelway's Coral Plume' produces coral-pink flowers opening from pure pink buds. The plume poppy's natural habitat is Chinese and Japanese meadows where it makes large impressive colonies, spreading quickly through the damp soil by underground rhizomes, flowering all summer long.

CONDITIONS

Aspect	Macleaya likes full sun and light shade, though the former produces a longer, better display. Avoid dark areas. Also avoid open windy sites; shelter is required.
Site	Light, well-drained soil is ideal.

GROWING METHOD

Propagation	The quickest, easiest results are either by making spring or autumn divisions, or by separating lengths of rhizome when the plant is dormant. Make sure each has its own root system. Water new plants well, and space out at 90cm (3ft) intervals.
Feeding	Provide moderate applications of compost and well-rotted manure in the spring as a mulch.
Problems	Colonies of slugs can be a severe problem, badly attacking the new, vigorous growth. Either pick off by hand or treat accordingly with chemicals.

FLOWERING

Season	Flowers appear in mid- and late summer on long, thin stems producing an airy display.
Cutting	Macleaya make very attractive cut flowers, requiring a regular change of water, their airy panicles adding considerably to both formal and flowery arrangements.

AFTER FLOWERING

Requirements Cut back old growth to the ground.

MACLEAYA AT A GLANCE

M. cordata is a rhizomatous perennial with grey-green foliage, grown for its tall flower spikes. Hardy to −18°C (0°F).

		COMPANION PLANTS
JAN	/	
FEB	/	Clematis
MAR	/	Gypsophila
APR	division	Hibiscus
MAY	/	Miscanthus
JUN	/	Lobelia
JULY	flowering	Osteospermum
AUG	flowering	Rose
SEPT	/	Salvia
OCT	division	
NOV	/	
DEC	/	

MECONOPSIS
Himalayan blue poppy

NO OTHER blue flower has quite the same startlingly clear colour as the amazing blue poppy, a true delight whenever it can be grown.

WOODLAND CONDITIONS where the soil never really dries out are essential for the Himalayan or Tibetan blue poppy.

FEATURES

SUMMER AUTUMN WINTER SPRING

HERBACEOUS

Meconopsis betonicifolia is the beautiful blue poppy everyone loves. There is probably no other plant that produces such an intense sky-blue flower. Its natural habitat is very high altitude alpine meadows in China. Plants do not flower the first year, and they die down in winter, growing and blooming the second year. If meconopsis is prevented from blooming the first time it sets buds, it is more likely to become perennial. Growing to almost 2m (6½ft) in its native habitat, in cultivation it is more likely to be 50–70cm (20–28in) high. Looks best when grown as part of a massed display, or threaded through a border.

MECONOPSIS AT A GLANCE

M. betonicifolia is a deciduous perennial, making a strong show, with blue or white, early summer flowers. Hardy to –18° (0°F).

		RECOMMENDED VARIETIES
JAN	/	
FEB	/	*Meconopsis cambrica*
MAR	sow	*M. betonicifolia*
APR	transplant	*M. grandis*
MAY	transplant	*M. napaulensis*
JUN	flowering	*M. quintuplinervia*
JULY	flowering	*M. x sheldonii*
AUG	flowering	*M. x s. 'Slieve Donard'*
SEPT	flowering	*M. superba*
OCT	sow	
NOV	/	
DEC	/	

CONDITIONS

Aspect   Needs partial, dappled shade; also provide some protection from strong, cutting, drying winds.

Site   Needs a well-drained soil that is rich in organic matter. In colder regions it grows best in acid soil.

GROWING METHOD

Propagation   Grows from fresh ripe seed sown in the autumn, or in spring. Give winter seedlings frost protection in a greenhouse, but beware of damping off, and plant out in late spring or early summer. Initially water well. Do not waterlog or the crowns will rot.

Feeding   Apply a little general fertiliser in the spring.

Problems   Overwet soil, especially during winter, will rot the crown. Downy mildew may be a problem in some seasons. Spray plants with a fungicide at the first sign of an attack.

FLOWERING

Season   Abundant flowers begin appearing at the start of summer.

Cutting   While they make extremely good cut flowers, they do not last that long.

AFTER FLOWERING

Requirements   Remove spent flower stems unless you are waiting for seed to ripen. Once growth dies down, cut it off at ground level.

MELIANTHUS MAJOR
Honey bush

NECTAR RICH, these dark red flowers are very attractive to insects. The foliage too, is unusual, with its distinctive colour and form.

THE BLUE-GREEN FOLIAGE of honey flower is a feature in itself. Only in a largish garden will you appreciate the full effect.

FEATURES

SUMMER AUTUMN WINTER SPRING
EVERGREEN

This very striking evergreen plant with its unusual blue-green foliage really stands out. It is grown as a feature in a mixed border or as a focal point in an annual or perennial display. In a large garden it could be repeat planted to tie together various arrangements. Honey bush can grow to 2m (6ft) in height, and it spreads by suckers, forming a large clump if left undivided. The dark mahogany-red flowers contain copious quantities of nectar, attractive to bees. Although native to South Africa, and initially tender here, after two years the base becomes woody and it can survive outside if given good frost protection in mild areas. It can also be grown in a large pot.

MELIANTHUS AT A GLANCE

M. major is a tender, southern African plant with wonderful, architectural foliage. It is damaged below 5°C (41°F).

		COMPANION PLANTS
JAN	/	
FEB	/	Canna
MAR	sow	Choisya
APR	divide	*Hosta* 'Krossa Regal'
MAY	transplant	Philadelphus
JUN	flowering	Pinus
JULY	flowering	Pseudopanax
AUG	flowering	Salvia
SEPT	/	
OCT	/	
NOV	/	
DEC	/	

CONDITIONS

Aspect Needs full sun all day (i.e. a south-facing wall).
Site Soil must be well drained but it need not be specially rich, in fact over-rich soils will produce good foliage effects but poor flowering. However, the outstanding architectural foliage is the main reason for growing this striking plant.

GROWING METHOD

Propagation Grows from seed sown in spring or from division of suckers on an existing plant, also in spring. Plant at least 1m (39in) apart. For best growth give deep watering every week or two in hot, dry spells during the growing season. It will, however, tolerate drought well.
Feeding Apply a complete plant food in spring.
Problems Red spider mites may strike. Use an appropriate insecticide.

FLOWERING

Season Dark crimson flowers may appear in late summer or earlier on long stems that survived the winter.
Cutting Flowers are probably best left on the plant as they do not smell particularly pleasant.

AFTER FLOWERING

Requirements Cut off the spent flower stems unless you are waiting for seed to set and ripen. Protect the base and roots with straw or bracken against frost. The older and woodier the plant, the better its chance of survival.

MIMULUS
Monkey flower

THE MONKEY FLOWER is an indispensable part of the cottage garden. It forms bright clumps, spreads within reason, never becoming invasive, and gives a long flowering season from spring to summer. It is ideal for a site near a pond, its shapes reflecting gently in the water.

FEATURES

HERBACEOUS

The genus has 150 species, and while they are classified as annuals, perennials and shrubs of varying degrees of hardiness, from the gardener's viewpoint most are grown as the first. *M. cardinalis,* scarlet monkey flower, however, is an attractive, reliable perennial. It grows 90cm (3ft) high, producing vertical stems with eye-catching, tubular scarlet flowers in summer. Clumps usually spread 60cm (24in). In the wild, from western North America down to Mexico, it is pollinated by humingbirds. *M. luteus,* monkey musk, has yellow flowers with a red throat, and self-seeds freely through the garden. *M. guttatus* has attractive, funnel-shape yellow flowers.

MIMULUS AT A GLANCE

Mimulus contains many ideal, damp garden plants, creating colonies with bright flowers. Several hardy to –15ºC (5ºF).

		RECOMMENDED VARIETIES
JAN	/	
FEB	/	*Mimulus aurantiacus*
MAR	divide	Calypso hybrids
APR	transplant	*M. cardinalis*
MAY	flowering	*M. c* 'Whitecroft Scarlet'
JUN	flowering	'Highland Red' '
JULY	flowering	*M. lewisii*
AUG	flowering	*M. ringens*
SEPT	/	
OCT	sow	
NOV	/	
DEC	/	

CONDITIONS

Aspect   Mimulus thrive in either full sun or light shade.

Site   Provide rich, moist soil. In their natural habitat many mimulus grow alongside streams and ponds. They are ideal for the bog garden or a running stream. However, *M. cardinalis* will tolerate drier ground.

GROWING METHOD

Propagation   Divide in spring, setting out vigorous new clumps up to 90cm (3ft) apart. Softwood cuttings can be taken in the early part of summer, while semi-ripe, slightly hardier ones can be taken after mid-summer. Sow seed in spring or autumn.

Feeding   Add plenty of well-rotted manure and compost, and a spring mulch to preserve moisture loss.

Problems   Slugs and snails can be a major problem, devouring tender new growth. Either pick them off by hand, trap and remove, or treat with a chemical.

FLOWERING

Season   The flowers appear from late spring to summer.

Cutting   Mimulus make good cut flowers, though they do not tend to last long. Regular, fresh supplies will be needed.

AFTER FLOWERING

Requirements   Cut back to ground level in late autumn, and remove the dead foliage which can prove a haven to slugs and snails.

MISCANTHUS SINENSIS
Miscanthus

FINE STRIPES in cream and green make 'Variegatus' a popular form of miscanthus.

ZEBRA GRASS is the common name given to 'Zebrinus', with its yellow-spotted horizontal markings. Ornamental grasses can provide useful contrast in the perennial garden.

FEATURES

SUMMER AUTUMN WINTER SPRING

HERBACEOUS

This is a group of large, ornamental, herbaceous perennial grasses. The plain green species is not often grown as the many cultivars with striped or banded foliage are much more decorative. Cultivars range in height from about 81cm (32in) to 2m (6½ft). Clumps spread from short, thick rhizomes and become very wide after a few years if not divided. Commonly grown cultivars include 'Zebrinus' with distinct, horizontal gold banding, and 'Variegatus' with long cream or white stripes, while other varieties such as 'Silberfeder', 'Morning Light' and var. *purpurascens* are worth seeking out. All produce pale, creamy beige feathery plumes of flowers in late summer, and autumn, often accompanied by good autumn colour. The tall growers look good crested with frost.

MISCANTHUS AT A GLANCE

M. sinensis is a deciduous, large perennial, growing 1.8 x 1.8m (6ft x 6ft). Produces blue-green foliage. Hardy to −18°C (0°F).

		RECOMMENDED VARIETIES
JAN	/	
FEB	sow	'Ferne Osten'
MAR	sow	'Flamingo'
APR	transplant	'Gracillimus'
MAY	divide	'Kleine Fontane'
JUN	/	'Kleine Silberspinne'
JULY	/	'Morning Light'
AUG	flowering	'Strictus'
SEPT	flowering	'Undine'
OCT	flowering	
NOV	/	
DEC	/	

CONDITIONS

Aspect Grows best in full sun, but tolerates shade for part of the day.

Site Prefers a soil that has been heavily enriched with organic matter to aid moisture retention. Avoid any damp or boggy ground. Good drainage really is essential for a massed, architectural display.

GROWING METHOD

Propagation Clumps can be lifted and divided in spring. This can require considerable muscle and effort because the roots are extremely tenacious. Replant the divisions approximately 30cm (12in) apart, or closer if you want quicker, immediate coverage. Water well until established.

Feeding Complete plant food can be applied in the spring, when new growth begins, but it is not essential if the soil contains plenty of manure or compost.

Problems No specific pest or disease problems are known to attack this plant.

FLOWERING

Season Flowering plumes appear well above the foliage in the autumn.

Cutting Plumes can be cut and dried like pampas grass.

AFTER FLOWERING

Requirements Once foliage starts to die off and become unsightly, cut it off at ground level. If the foliage is left uncut to provide winter shapes and outlines, especially when frosted, it must be cut back by early spring.

MONARDA DIDYMA

Bergamot

THE HOT-PINK FLOWERS on this bergamot are easy to place in the garden. They combine well with blue or white schemes.

FOR COLOUR over a long period, this brilliant red variety of bergamot, 'Cambridge Scarlet', is hard to beat. It requires little care.

FEATURES

SUMMER AUTUMN WINTER SPRING

HERBACEOUS

This is an aromatic herbaceous perennial which is also known as bee balm and Oswego tea. The name bee balm refers to its nectar-rich flowers, which are very attractive to bees, and Oswego tea to its use by the Oswego Indians and early colonists of North America as a tea substitute. Growing about 90cm (36in) high, bergamot flowers from mid- to late summer. The heads of tubular flowers are red, pink, white or purple with some outstanding named cultivars, including 'Cambridge Scarlet' and 'Croftway Pink'. It is easy to grow. Being a member of the mint family its roots spread vigorously, but it makes a lively addition to a mixed planting for its bright scarlet or pink flowers.

MONARDA AT A GLANCE

M. didyma is a clump-forming perennial with lance-shape leaves, and bright late summer flowers. Hardy to −18ºC (0ºF).

JAN	/	RECOMMENDED VARIETIES
FEB	sow	'Aquarius'
MAR	sow	'Beauty of Cobham'
APR	transplant	'Cambridge Scarlet'
MAY	transplant	'Croftway Pink'
JUN	/	'Fishes'
JULY	flowering	'Mahogany'
AUG	flowering	'Prarienacht'
SEPT	/	'Sagittarius'
OCT	sow	'Scorpion'
NOV	/	
DEC	/	

CONDITIONS

Aspect Grows in either full sun or semi-shade, but flowering will be best in the open.

Site Needs well-drained soil that is made moisture retentive by the addition of large amounts of decayed organic matter.

GROWING METHOD

Propagation Lift and divide clumps in spring before new growth begins. Replant the young, vigorous outer growths 20–30cm (8–12in) apart. Plants usually need dividing every two or three years. Bergamot may be also be grown from seed sown either in the early spring or autumn, but this does not come true to type. Needs regular, deep watering through prolonged dry spells in the heat of summer.

Feeds If the soil is well supplied with humus, but a little fertiliser is needed. Apply some complete plant food in the spring.

Problems Since snails love to eat the new growth as it appears, take precautions. Mildew can be a problem at times. You may need a fungicide spray or it might become severe. Remove all dead and diseased leaves.

FLOWERING

Season Flowers in mid- and late summer.

Cutting Makes a decent cut flower. Use the scented leaves in a pot-pourri.

AFTER FLOWERING

Requirements Prune off spent flower stems. Cut plants back to ground level once growth begins to die off.

OENOTHERA
Evening primrose

THOUGH EVENING PRIMROSE is thought of as yellow, the flowers of Oenothera speciosa 'Rosea' are pink and white, with yellow.

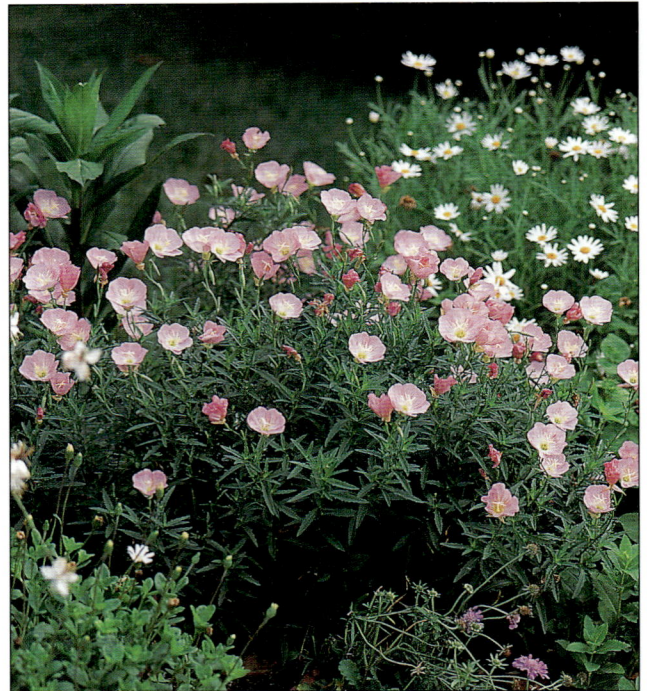

O. SPECIOSA 'ROSEA' is doubly attractive because it grows 30cm (12in) high, mixes well with argyranthemum, and forms large clumps.

FEATURES

Evening primrose is an essential plant for formal and cottage-style gardens. While each flower (white, yellow or pink, depending on variety) opens and fades fast, barely lasting 24 hours, there is an abundance of new buds developing through summer and early autumn. The plant has two extra advantages. Often fragrant, and often tall, it can make an eye-catching addition to the border. *O. biennis,* the traditional favourite is actually an annual or biennial. *O. fruticosa,* a biennial or perennial, has two fine forms, 'Fyrverkeri' ('Fireworks')

which has red buds opening to yellow flowers and purple-tinged leaves, and subsp. *glauca,* with yellow flowers and purple leaves.

CONDITIONS

Aspect Grow in an open, sunny position.
Site Moderately rich soil will suffice, though evening primrose can self-seed and appear in even the stoniest ground.

GROWING METHOD

Propagation Sow seed or divide in early spring, or take cuttings of non-flowering shoots. Keep in a frost-free place in winter, plant out in spring.
Feeding Not necessary, though moderate quantities of manure will suffice in especially poor soil.
Problems Slugs tend to be the main problem, attacking tender new growth. Pick off or treat with chemicals. The sturdy kinds of evening primrose are free-standing, but others (*O. macrocarpa*) may require support.

FLOWERING

Season Lasts from late spring to late summer, with flowers tending to open in early evening when they release their scent.
Cutting Short-lived but attractive flowers.

AFTER FLOWERING

Requirements Collect seed when ripe, if required, and then cut spent stems to the ground.

OENOTHERA AT A GLANCE

A genus of mainly annuals and biennials, with excellent perennials. Scented and yellow flowering they are hardy to −15°C (5°F).

		RECOMMENDED VARIETIES
JAN	/	
FEB	sow	*Oenothera biennis*
MAR	divide	*O. fruticosa*
APR	transplant	*O. f.* 'Fyrverkeri'
MAY	flowering	*O. f.* subsp. *glauca*
JUN	flowering	*O. macrocarpa*
JULY	flowering	*O. speciosa* 'Rosea'
AUG	flowering	*O. stricta* 'Sulphurea'
SEPT	/	
OCT	/	
NOV	/	
DEC	/	

PAEONIA
Paeony species and cultivars

GLORIOUS COLOUR and perfume combine in this extensive planting of peony cultivars to produce a spectacular result.

THIS HALF-OPENED peony flower gives a hint of delights to come, with a touch of white against the bright pink.

FLUTED PETALS give extra interest to this single white peony. The large mass of central stamens adds a touch of colour.

FEATURES

HERBACEOUS

Beautiful to look at and fragrant too, peonies are among the aristocrats of the plant world, and although there are only 33 wild species, there are many hundreds of cultivars. Peonies were prized by the Chinese for many hundreds of years, and by the early 18th century they had developed the garden peonies from which the forms of *P. lactiflora* (often referred to as Chinese peonies) are generally descended. Peonies were first introduced into Europe at the end of the 18th century. Peonies are divided into two groups: the tree peonies, which are shrubby and derived from *P. suffruticosa*, and the herbaceous peonies, of which the cultivars of *P. lactiflora* are most commonly grown. Although the name 'tree peony' is used this is an exaggeration, they rarely grow more than 2m (6½ft) high. Herbaceous peonies grow about 1m (39in) high and wide. Plants are long lived.

Flowers Flowers may be single or double and come in every shade of pink, red, purple, white and cream, many with a delicious light perfume. Some flowers have a large central boss of golden stamens, and some have fringed or crimped edges on the petals. Among the categories of flowers recognised are: small, 5–10cm (2–4in) across; medium, 10–15cm, (4–6in); large, 15–20cm (6–8in); and very large, over 20cm (8in). Tree peonies are generally 5–30cm (2–12in). Other categories have been developed in the United States where a great deal of hybridising is practised.

CONDITIONS

Aspect Needs full sun or semi-shade with protection from strong winds.

Site Soil must be well drained, but heavily enriched with manure or compost. Dig it over deeply to allow the free spread of the roots.

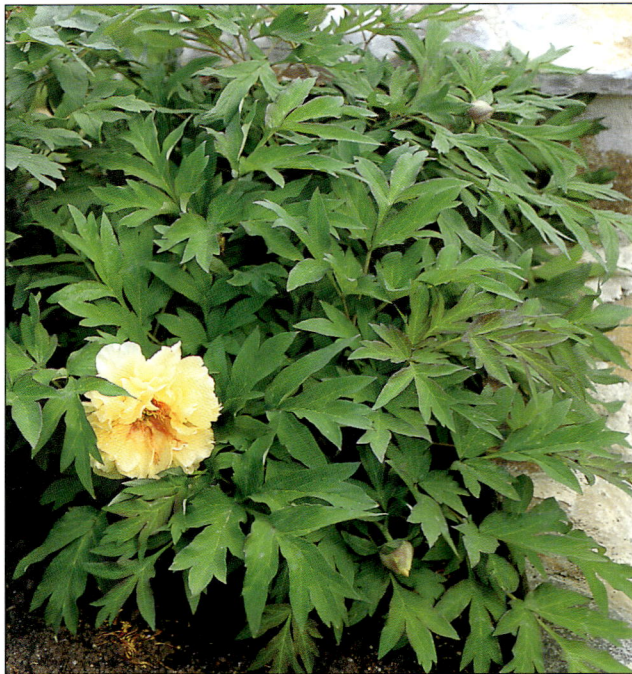

THE ATTRACTIVE FOLIAGE greatly adds to the value of peonies and often emerges with lovely rich red and bronze tints.

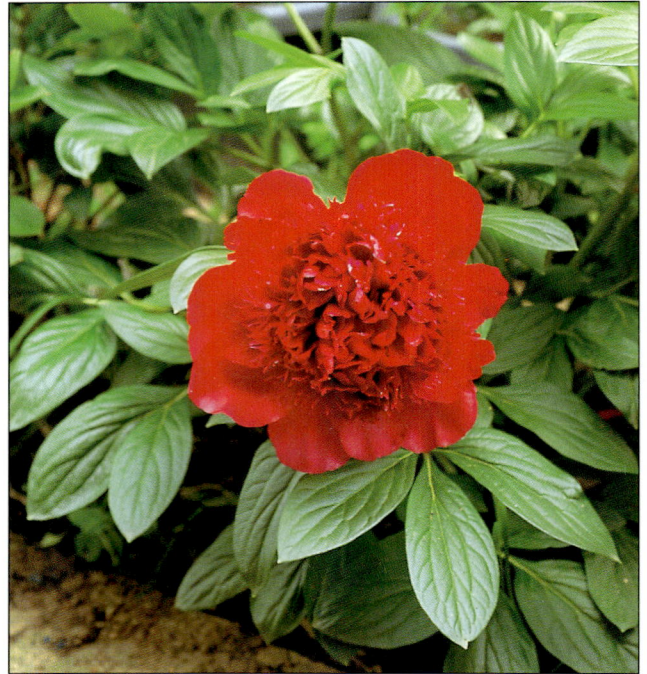

THE VERY POPULAR double cultivar 'Rubra Plena' is a rich crimson anemone-centred peony that looks very like a camellia.

GROWING METHOD

Propagation Divide plants in the spring or autumn, taking care not to break the brittle roots. Each division must have roots and dormant growth buds. Crowns should be replanted 2.5cm (1in) below the surface, and spaced about 50cm (20in) apart. Plants can be raised from seed but they will take four to five years to reach flowering size, and only the species will be true to type. Peony seeds generally need two periods of chilling with a warm period between, and care should be taken not to disturb the seeds during this time. Most seeds germinate the second spring after sowing.

Feeding Apply a general fertiliser in early spring. At the same time mulch but avoid the crown.

PAEONIA AT A GLANCE

A genus of over 30 species of clump-forming perennials and sub-shrubs, often with highly scented flowers. Hardy to −15°C (5°F).

		RECOMMENDED VARIETIES
JAN	/	
FEB	/	*P. cambessedesii*
MAR	/	'Defender'
APR	divide 🌿	*P. lactiflora* 'Bowl of Beauty'
MAY	transplant 🌿	
JUN	flowering 🌸	*P. l.* 'Festiva Maxima'
JULY	/	*P. l.* 'Sarah Bernhardt'
AUG	/	*P. mlokosewitschii*
SEPT	/	*P. obovata*
OCT	sow 🌱	
NOV	sow 🌱	
DEC	sow 🌱	

Problems Botrytis or grey mould is the main problem with peonies. It can cause rotting of stems and leaf bases. Destroy affected foliage, improve drainage and air circulation, and spray with a fungicide. Replace the top layer of soil carefully around the plants.

FLOWERING

Season The flowering period is invariably early summer. Some peonies bloom for only a short time, but the flowers on other types are much longer lasting.

Cutting Cut flowers for indoor use just as the blooms are opening. Peonies are excellent cut flowers, which will last longer if kept in a cool part of the house and given frequent water changes.

AFTER FLOWERING

Requirements Remove spent flower stems but allow the foliage to die down naturally before trimming it back. Some varieties produce lovely autumn colour. Do not to cut down the flowering stems of varieties such as *P. mlokosewitschii* that produce handsome berries.

HINT

Disturbance Peonies may flower poorly, if at all, the first year after planting, but this should improve year by year. Generally speaking, peonies are best left undisturbed; even 50-year-old clumps can be seen flowering profusely. You may be wiser to increase your stock by buying young container-grown plants than split a precious specimen.

PAPAVER ORIENTALE
Oriental poppy

THIS FRINGED red flower indicates the wide range of colours within P. orientale. *No border should be without one.*

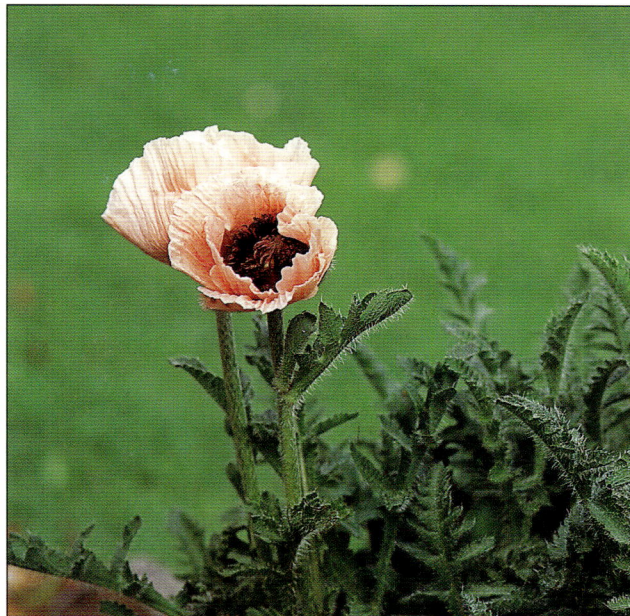

THE STRIKING SHAPE of Papaver orientale. *Note the straight, slightly furry stem with, here, pink flowers and a black basal mark.*

FEATURES

SUMMER AUTUMN WINTER SPRING
HERBACEOUS

The oriental poppy is a clump-forming perennial with a variety of different forms, and colours ranging from soft hues to sharp red. They all bear the hallmarks of the species, *P. orientalis,* from north-east Turkey and Iran, which has a large cupped bowl of a flower with paper thin petals. Growing up to 90cm (36in) tall, with a similar spread, they self-seed freely, creating attractive colonies. They look the part in both wild, or natural gardens, and large mixed borders. 'Black and White' is a striking contrast of white petals and a black mark at its base. 'Cedric Morris' is soft pink with a black base. 'Indian Chief' is reddish-brown.

PAPAVER AT A GLANCE

P. orientalis is a perennial with 30cm (12in) long leaves, and big, cupped flowers in a range of colours. Hardy to −18°C (0°F).

		RECOMMENDED VARIETIES
JAN	/	
FEB	/	*Papaver orientale* 'Allegro'
MAR	/	*P. o.* 'Beauty of Livermere'
APR	division	*P. o.* 'Black and White'
MAY	flowering	*P. o.* Goliath Group
JUN	flowering	*P. o.* 'Mrs Perry'
JULY	flowering	*P. o.* 'Patty's Plum'
AUG	/	*P. o.* 'Perry's White'
SEPT	/	*P. o.* 'Picotee'
OCT	sow	*P. o.* 'Turkish Delight'
NOV	/	
DEC	/	

CONDITIONS

Aspect   Provide full sun, the conditions it receives in its natural habitat.

Site   Rich soil and good drainage bring out the best in these plants.

GROWING METHOD

Propagation   Since they self-seed freely, propagation may not be necessary. Slicing off sections of root in late autumn or early winter will provide abundant new plants. The success rate is invariably high. Alternatively, divide clumps in the spring, or sow seed in pots in the autumn in a cold frame. Plant out the following spring, 23cm (9in) apart.

Feeding   Add plenty of rich, friable compost in spring to add fertility to poor soils, also improving the drainage which needs to be quite good.

Problems   Fungal wilt and downy mildew can be problems; spray at the first sign.

FLOWERING

Season   The flowers appear from late spring to mid-summer.

Cutting   Poppies do not make good cut flowers.

AFTER FLOWERING

Requirements   When the flowers have died down, severely cut back the foliage to the ground. This will produce a second showing of attractive summer leaves.

PENSTEMON
Beard tongue

MANY MONTHS of fine bloom can be expected from this fine red cultivar, well into autumn, if it is regularly deadheaded.

A GENEROUS PLANTING of these attractive white cultivars makes a perfect surround for this small ornamental fountain.

FEATURES

SUMMER AUTUMN WINTER SPRING
EVERGREEN

This very large group of perennials consists of 250 species and countless cultivars, all originating in a wide variety of habitats in the southern and western United States. Their tubular or funnel-shaped flowers come in a range of shades of pink, red, purple, lavender, blue and white, some with a contrasting throat. There is a large range of cultivars in many of these shades. Collections can also be bought as young rooted cuttings. Penstemons have a long flowering period through summer to mid-autumn, especially if the spent blooms are regularly cut, but many plants can be short-lived. Take cuttings regularly. The various species and hybrids grow anything from 10cm–60cm (4–24in) high.

PENSTEMON AT A GLANCE

A large genus of perennials grown for their late-season flower display. Hardiness varies from the frost tender to –15ºC (5ºF).

		RECOMMENDED VARIETIES
JAN	/	
FEB	sow 🖐	'Alice Hindley'
MAR	sow 🖐	'Beech Park'
APR	transplant 🖐	'Chester Scarlet'
MAY	transplant 🖐	'Evelyn'
JUN	flowering 🌺	'Garnet'
JULY	flowering 🌺	'Margery Fish'
AUG	flowering 🌺	'Osprey'
SEPT	flowering 🌺	'Pennington Gem'
OCT	flowering 🌺	'Rubicundus'
NOV	/	
DEC	/	

CONDITIONS

Aspect Grows best in full sun with some protection from strong, cutting winds. Since most varieties are not fully hardy, warmth and shelter are essential.

Site Needs very open, and well-drained soil.

GROWING METHOD

Propagation They grow well from cuttings taken mid-summer, then overwintered in a greenhouse frame. A wide range of penstemons can also be grown from seed which is widely available. They need a cold period before germination; sow in the autumn or refrigerate the seed for three weeks before sowing in the spring.

Feeding Apply a general fertiliser as new growth commences in the spring.

Problems No specific pest or disease problems, but root rot may occur on sticky clay soil.

FLOWERING

Season Most have a fairly long flowering period from summer to mid-autumn. However, many can only be seen as true perennials in milder parts of the country, being killed by winter frosts; raise new stock to replace any losses. 'Garnet' is the hardiest.

Cutting This is not a satisfactory cut flower.

AFTER FLOWERING

Requirements Either cut entirely to the ground, or leave some stems as frost protection. Protect clumps with a mulch of straw or bracken.

PHLOX PANICULATA
Perennial phlox

THE ATTRACTIVE, *individual flowers on the heads of perennial phlox last right through the season, making it essential in any border.*

A GREAT STANDBY *for the summer garden, perennial phlox fills the whole of the back of this border with two shades of pink.*

FEATURES

HERBACEOUS

Easy to grow and producing a summer-long display of flowers, perennial phlox has a place in any perennial collection. Plants may grow from 40–90cm (16–36in) high, and the clumps spread rapidly; space new plantings 30cm (12in) apart. The large heads of flowers, some with a contrasting eye, come in shades of red, pink, orange, mauve, purple and white. This plant looks best mass planted, either in solid blocks of one colour or in mixed colours. Also note the highly popular, new variegated cultivars. With mixed plantings ensure that the taller forms do not obscure the shorter ones.

PHLOX AT A GLANCE

P. paniculata is an erect, herbaceous perennial with scented flowers, and many excellent cultivars. Hardy to −15°C (5°F).

		RECOMMENDED VARIETIES
JAN	/	*Phlox paniculata* 'Alba
FEB	sow	Grandiflora'
MAR	sow	*P. p.* 'Blue Ice'
APR	transplant	*P. p.* 'Bumble's Delight'
MAY	transplant	*P. p.* 'Eventide'
JUN		*P. p.* 'Le Mahdi'
JULY	flowering	*P. p.* 'Prince of Orange'
AUG	flowering	*P. p.* 'Prospero'
SEPT	flowering	*P. p.* 'White Admiral'
OCT	divide	
NOV	/	
DEC	/	

CONDITIONS

Aspect Prefers full sun with some protection from strong wind.
Site Needs a well-drained soil enriched with organic matter.

GROWING METHOD

Propagation Divide clumps in the autumn every three or four years, making sure that each division has a crown and a decent set of roots. Replant only the younger, vigorous outer growths, discarding the rest. Plants propagated from root cuttings will be free of eelworm.
Feeding Apply a complete plant food in spring and mulch well with rotted manure or compost, but do not cover the crowns.
Problems Powdery mildew can be a problem. Spray with a fungicide. Phlox eelworm causes leaves to shrivel, and shrubs distort. Plants must be destroyed.

FLOWERING

Season From summer into early autumn.
Cutting It makes a good cut flower.

AFTER FLOWERING

Requirements Remove spent flower stems as they fade. In late autumn cut off any remaining growth. Give the plants a thorough tidy up for the winter.

PHYSOSTEGIA VIRGINIANA
Obedient plant

THE SHORT SPIKES of flowers are attached to the obedient plant by a joint so that they can be rearranged as you please.

OBEDIENT PLANT looks best in large plantings and it is well worth devoting garden space to it as the flowers last for several months.

FEATURES

HERBACEOUS

This is an easy-care, fast-growing perennial. Since it spreads by stolons (runners) and seed, large clumps can develop in one season. Excess plants are quite easily removed. The dark green leaves are only 10–15cm (4–6in) high, but flowering stems bring the height up to 1.2m (4ft). The flowers in the species are pinky mauve, but there are cultivars with flowers in various shades of pink, red and white. It looks best planted in large drifts in a border, or among shrubs. The common name refers to the fact that flowers remain fixed the way they are turned. It is also sometimes known as false dragon's head.

PHYSOSTEGIA AT A GLANCE

P. virginiana is a spreading, tall perennial with purple or lilac-tinged flowers lasting into autumn. Hardy to 0°C (32°F).

		RECOMMENDED VARIETIES
JAN	/	
FEB	/	*Physostegia virginiana* 'Alba'
MAR	divide	*P. v.* 'Crown of Snow'
APR	transplant	*P. v.* 'Red Beauty'
MAY	transplant	*P. v.* 'Summer Snow'
JUN	/	*P. v.* 'Vivid'
JULY	flowering	*P. v.* subsp. *speciosa*
AUG	flowering	'Bouquet Rose'
SEPT	flowering	
OCT	sow	
NOV	/	
DEC	/	

CONDITIONS

Aspect   Grows well in both full sun and semi-shade. However, some form of protection from strong winds is desirable. The taller varieties may need staking.

Site   Tolerates a wide range of soils, but the best results are when grown in well-drained soil, rich in organic matter.

GROWING METHOD

Propagation   Divide old clumps in spring, planting new divisions in groups for the best effect. The oldest sections can be discarded. Because of its vigorous habit you need to divide every couple of years. Tolerates dry periods well, but you must water young plants regularly until they are established.

Feeding   Apply a complete plant food in spring. Mulch with decayed organic matter at the same time.

Problems   No specific problems are known.

FLOWERING

Season   Flowers appear from mid- to late summer into the autumn.

Cutting   Frequent cutting of blooms should produce a second flush of flowers. Scald cut stems to prolong their vase life.

AFTER FLOWERING

Requirements Remove spent flower stems and tidy up growth as it dies down.

PLATYCODON
Balloon flower

THE BUDS of platycodon swell into a balloon-shape, hence the common name, then pop open revealing these beautiful flowers.

THIS WELL-ESTABLISHED CLUMP of balloon flower is supported by stakes guaranteeing height as well as colour.

FEATURES

HERBACEOUS

Also known as Chinese bellflower, this herbaceous perennial grows around 50cm (20in) high, slightly taller in perfect conditions. It has a shortish flowering period in late summer, and the open, bell-shape flowers come in a range of blue shades, but also in white and pale pink. Flowers last well when cut. There are several named cultivars available, including double and semi-double ones. Since clumps are compact and spread slowly, they are best planted where they can remain undisturbed for some years. The new growth appears in late spring; mark its position to avoid hauling it out as a weed.

PLATYCODON AT A GLANCE

P. grandiflorus is a one-specie genus grown for its beautiful purple-blue flowers. Several fine cultivars. Hardy to −15ºC (5ºF).

		COMPANION PLANTS
JAN	/	
FEB	/	Aster
MAR	sow	Clematis
APR	divide	Dahlia
MAY	transplant	Fuchsia
JUN	/	Osteospermum
JULY	/	Phygelius
AUG	flowering	*Rhodochiton atrosanguineus*
SEPT	flowering	Rose
OCT	/	
NOV	/	
DEC	/	

CONDITIONS

Aspect Grows in sun or dappled sunlight.
Site Grows best in a well-drained soil enriched with plenty of organic matter.

GROWING METHOD

Propagation Seed is the best means of propagation; sow in the spring. Young shoots can be taken as cuttings, and the double forms must be grown from cuttings. Also, clumps can be lifted and divided in the spring; replant the divisions about 20–25cm (8–10in) apart. Give newly bedded plants a regular watering during prolonged dry spells in the spring and summer.

Feeding Apply a complete plant food when the new growth begins to appear in the spring.

Problems Slugs can be a major problem devouring new growth. Either pick off by hand or treat chemically.

FLOWERING

Season A relatively short display, which is more than compensated for by the nature of the exquisite flowers.

Cutting Flowers can be cut for the vase.

AFTER FLOWERING

Requirements Cut right back to the ground all spent flower stems, and then the whole plant as the growth dies off.

POLYGONATUM
Solomon's seal

A HORIZONTAL STEM of pretty white Solomon's seal flowers is suspended above a groundcover of lungwort and dead nettle.

SOLOMON'S SEAL grows tall in the dappled shade of this garden, where it is teamed with hostas, lady's mantle and foxgloves.

FEATURES

HERBACEOUS

This lovely herbaceous perennial is ideal for naturalising in the dappled shade of a garden. The plant has a graceful, arching habit with stems 60–90 cm (24–36in) long. The finely veined foliage tends to stand up on the stem, while the tubular white bell flowers hang down. It grows from a creeping rhizome and will spread to form a colony of plants given the right conditions. If space is no problem, plant several to start your display, letting them form large colonies. A number of other species are grown, some, such as *P. odoratum*, with scented flowers. 'Flore Pleno' has double flowers. There are two variegated, eye-catching forms.

POLYGONATUM AT A GLANCE

P. x *hybridum* (*multiflorum*) is a rhizomatous perennial with green-tipped white flowers; black fruit. Hardy to –18°C° (0°F).

		RECOMMENDED VARIETIES
JAN	/	
FEB	/	*P. biflorum*
MAR	divide	*P. falcatum*
APR	transplant	*P. f.* 'Variegatum'
MAY	flowering	*P. hookeri*
JUN	/	*P. odoratum* 'Flore Pleno'
JULY	/	*P. verticillatum*
AUG	/	
SEPT	/	
OCT	sow	
NOV	/	
DEC	/	

CONDITIONS

Aspect Needs a sheltered spot in part or full shade.
Site The soil should drain well but be heavily enriched with organic matter to retain some moisture at all times. The plants benefit from an early spring mulch.

GROWING METHOD

Propagation Established clumps can be divided in early spring, new divisions being spaced 20–25cm (8–10in) apart. This plant is best left undisturbed for several years if possible. Young plants need to be watered regularly during the growing season; do not let them dry out.
Feeding Apply complete plant food as new growth commences in spring.
Problems Plants can be severely devastated by attacks of sawfly larvae, which reduce them to skeletons. Either treat with a spray, or pick off the caterpillars.

FLOWERING

Season Flowers appear in late spring.
Cutting Flowers can be cut for indoor decoration. They last fairly well and make a good display.

AFTER FLOWERING

Requirements Do not cut down the flower stems or you will end up weakening the plant, and consequently losing the attractive, yellow autumn tints.

POTENTILLA
Cinquefoil

A SMART RED AND WHITE MIX of cinquefoil with annual heartsease, or Viola tricolor, *growing through it.*

DESPITE THE SMALL FLOWERS, these bright little plants are difficult to overlook in any perennial garden.

FEATURES

There are over 500 species of cinquefoil, including annuals, perennials and small shrubs. All have the characteristic five-lobed leaf, and the single or double flowers may be white or in shades of yellow, red or pink. Cinquefoil belongs to the rose family, and the foliage can be attractive even when plants are not in flower. They may be from 5–50cm (2–20in) or more high. The short types make good edging plants, while the taller ones can be used successfully in a mixed planting. Since flower stems tend to flop over they may need light support. Many red cinquefoils are hybrids of *P. atrosanguinea,* while some yellows derive from *P. argyrophylla* and *P. recta.* Some cinquefoils tend to self-seed.

POTENTILLA AT A GLANCE

A 500-species genus, mainly of herbaceous perennials and shrubs. An excellent colour range. Hardy to –18ºC (0ºF).

		RECOMMENDED VARIETIES
JAN	/	
FEB	/	*Potentilla cuneata*
MAR	sow	'Gibson's Scarlet'
APR	transplant	*P. megalantha*
MAY	transplant	*P. nepalensis* 'Miss
JUN	flowering	Willmott'
JULY	flowering	'William Rollison'
AUG	flowering	
SEPT	flowering	
OCT	sow	
NOV	/	
DEC	/	

CONDITIONS

Aspect   While it needs full sun it will also tolerate some dappled shade.

Site   Needs well-drained soil enriched with some organic matter.

GROWING METHOD

Propagation   Species and single-flowered varieties grow from both seed and cuttings. Sow the seed in early to mid-spring. The hybrid doubles must be grown from divisions taken during the spring or autumn, or you can use spring cuttings. The plant spacing depends on ultimate size, and may be anywhere from 15–40cm (6–16in).

Feeding   Apply a complete plant food as new growth commences in the spring.

Problems   Since these plants can easily flower themselves to death, propagate regularly to ensure you always have a good supply.

FLOWERING

Season   Flowers may begin in late spring in warm spells, but the main flowering period is during the summer months. Give the plant a light trim in early spring to force plenty of new growth and buds.

Cutting   Flowers do not last well when cut.

AFTER FLOWERING

Requirements   Cut off spent flower stems at ground level, and tidy up the plants as the growth dies off. In milder areas the foliage may hang on.

PRIMULA VULGARIS
Primrose

A CARPET OF PALE YELLOW PRIMROSES is one of the finest ways of announcing the arrival of spring in the garden. Given a cool, sheltered spot they will thrive and multiply year by year, even if they receive remarkably little attention.

FEATURES

HERBACEOUS

This is the true primrose of European woodlands. The species generally has soft, pale yellow flowers tucked in among the leaves on very short stalks, though occasionally white or pale pink forms are found. Cultivars come in a huge range of colours with single or double flowers, some on short stalks, others on quite tall ones. Primroses look their best mass planted under deciduous trees, or in drifts at the front of a lightly shaded bed or border. They can also be grown well in pots. Plants grow from about 10–15cm (4–6in) high, with flowering stems about the same height.

PRIMULA AT A GLANCE

P. vulgaris is an evergreen or semi-evergreen with scented, spring, generally pale yellow flowers. Hardy to –15°C (5°F).

JAN	/	
FEB	sow 🖐	
MAR	flowering 🌱	
APR	flowering 🌱	
MAY	flowering 🌱	
JUN	/	
JULY	/	
AUG	/	
SEPT	sow 🖐	
OCT	divide 🖐	
NOV	/	
DEC	/	

RECOMMENDED VARIETIES

'Ken Dearman'

'Miss Indigo'

Primula vulgaris 'Lilacina Plena'

P. v. subsp. *sibthorpii*

'Wanda'

CONDITIONS

Aspect Prefers to grow in semi-shade, and must have protection from the summer sun.

Site Grows best in a medium to heavy moisture-retentive soil, heavily enriched with organic matter. Mulch around the plants in spring.

GROWING METHOD

Propagation Lift and divide the crowns after flowering, in late autumn, and replant about 10–15cm (4–6in) apart. Sow your own seed when ripe (from late spring to early autumn); sow bought seed in early spring. Do not let young plants dry out.

Feeding Little fertiliser is needed if the soil is well enriched with plenty of humus, but a little general fertiliser in early spring gives an extra boost.

Problems Generally trouble free.

FLOWERING

Season Flowering usually lasts for several weeks during the spring. Deadheading prolongs the blooming. Massed displays look best.

Cutting Makes a fine posy, mixed with a range of more, early spring miniatures.

AFTER FLOWERING

Requirements In suitable conditions plants may self-seed. Remove dead leaves around the plant base.

PRIMULA SPECIES
Candelabra primulas

PRIMULA PULVERULENTA *happily combine here with hostas, both enjoying the damp conditions of a bog garden.*

THE CHARACTERISTIC TIERS *of flowers are well displayed in this healthy clump of white perennial primulas.*

FEATURES

HERBACEOUS

EVERGREEN

Candelabra primulas, which produce their flowers in distinct whorls or tiers up the stems, form one group among the several hundred species of primula. Most are herbaceous, but *P. helodoxa*, which has clear yellow flowers, is evergreen. Other species in this group include *P. aurantiaca*, *P. bulleyana*, *P. japonica* and *P. pulverulenta*. Flowers may be white, or in shades of yellow, orange, pink, red and purple. Plant heights vary from 30cm–1m (24–39in). These are plants that need to be placed in big groups for maximum impact. They need damp soil, being often planted around ponds and water features. Given the right conditions these plants will give a great show every year.

PRIMULA AT A GLANCE

Candelabra primulas are deciduous or semi-evergreen, flower on tall stems, and brighten up damp areas. Hardy to -15°C (5°F).

JAN	/	
FEB	sow 🌱	
MAR	sow 🌱	
APR	flowering 🌸	
MAY	flowering 🌸	
JUN	/	
JULY	/	
AUG	/	
SEPT	sow 🌱	
OCT	divide 🌱	
NOV	/	
DEC	/	

RECOMMENDED VARIETIES

Primula beesiana
P. bulleyana
'Inverewe'
P. japonica
Pagoda Hybrids
P. japonica
P. pulverulenta

CONDITIONS

Aspect Thrives in dappled shade.
Site Needs deep, moisture-retentive soil that is heavily enriched with organic matter, but it clearly dislikes being waterlogged over the winter months.

GROWING METHOD

Propagation Lift and divide the crowns after flowering, in late autumn, and replant about 10–15cm (4–6in) apart. Sow your own seed when ripe (from late spring to early autumn); sow bought seed in early spring. Do not let young plants dry out.
Feeding Little fertiliser is needed if the soil is well enriched with plenty of humus, but a scattering of general fertiliser in early spring gives an extra boost.
Problems Generally trouble free.

FLOWERING

Season This charming, essential garden primula flowers during the spring.
Cutting Flowers probably last a few days in the vase, and they add considerable charm to any arrangement, but the massed garden display will be the more rewarding.

AFTER FLOWERING

Requirements Spent flower stems can be cut off, unless you are waiting for seed to set. In good conditions many of the species will self-seed.

PULMONARIA
Lungwort

FLOWERING PULMONARIA are an essential feature of the spring garden.

THE SPOTTED FOLIAGE of lungwort makes a dense and attractive groundcover under trees. It is a reliable grower as long as it gets regular water in the spring and summer.

FEATURES

HERBACEOUS

EVERGREEN

Lungwort is well suited to planting under trees, between shrubs or at the front of a shady border. The abundant flowers appear before the leaves have fully developed, and are mostly in shades of blue, pink, and white. The foliage is very handsome, often silver spotted, and if sheared over after flowering produces a second, fresh mound of leaves. The whole plant is rarely more than 25–30cm (10–12in) high, and when established is very decorative, even out of flower. The plant gets its common name from the similarity between a spotted leaf and a diseased lung.

PULMONARIA AT A GLANCE

A genus of 14 species of deciduous and evergreen perennials. A flowering spreader for damp shade. Hardy to −18°C (0°F).

Jan	/	
Feb	/	
Mar	flowering	
Apr	flowering	
May	flowering	
Jun	divide	
July	/	
Aug	/	
Sept	/	
Oct	divide	
Nov	/	
Dec	/	

RECOMMENDED VARIETIES

Pulmonaria angustifolia
P. a. 'Munstead Blue'
P. longifolia 'Bertram Anderson'
P. officinalis Cambridge Blue Group
P. o. 'Sissinghurst White'
P. rubra
P. saccharata Argentea Group

CONDITIONS

Aspect Grows best in light shade, or in borders that are shady during the hottest part of the day. The leaves quickly wilt under a hot sun.

Site The soil should be heavily enriched with decayed organic matter, but it also needs to drain quite well.

GROWING METHOD

Propagation Grows from ripe seed, or by division of clumps either after flowering or in the autumn. Replant divisions about 15cm (6in) apart. Better still, let plants freely hybridise. Young and established plants need moist soil during the growing season.

Feeding Apply a little complete fertiliser in early spring and mulch well.

Problems No specific problems are known.

FLOWERING

Season Lungworts flower in the spring.

Cutting Flowers last quite well in a vase.

AFTER FLOWERING

Requirements Spent flowers can be cut off if you do not want seeding to occur. After the flowers have finished the foliage can be cut back to produce new fresh growth for the summer. Otherwise, little attention is required until the autumn, when the foliage can be tidied up as it fades.

PULSATILLA VULGARIS
Pasque flower

FOLK MEDICINE *makes use of the pasque flower, but it should be treated with caution as it can be fatal if used incorrectly.*

LIGHT FROST *here coats buds of the pasque flower, showing up the silky hairs. They will be more obvious on the seedheads.*

FEATURES

HERBACEOUS

The soft purple flowers appear before the leaves on this small, spring-flowering perennial. The whole plant is covered with silky hairs, giving it a delicate appearance that belies its hardy nature. After the petals have fallen, a decorative seedhead forms. The finely divided leaves grow from 10–15cm (4–6in) long, while the flowers may be on stems from 10–30cm (4–12in) high. Pasque flower should be planted in groups or drifts to get the best effect. There are now pink, white and red forms available. Since the leaves and flowers may cause skin irritation, wear gloves when handling if you have sensitive skin.

PULSATILLA AT A GLANCE

P. vulgaris is an attractive, clump-forming perennial with bell-like, silky flowers in shades of purple. Hardy to −18°C (0°F).

		RECOMMENDED VARIETIES
JAN	/	*Pulsatilla alpina* subsp.
FEB	/	*apiifolia*
MAR	/	P. *halleri*
APR	flowering	P. *halleri* subsp. *slavica*
MAY	flowering	P. *vernalis*
JUN	flowering	P. *vulgaris*
JULY	sow	P. *v.* 'Eva Constance'
AUG	sow	P. *v.* var. *rubra*
SEPT	/	
OCT	divide	
NOV	/	
DEC	/	

CONDITIONS

Aspect Prefers full sun but tolerates some semi-shade.

Site Needs very well-drained, gritty soil, rich in organic matter. They thrive on lime.

GROWING METHOD

Propagation Divide existing clumps after the foliage has died down, and then replant the divisions about 15–20cm (6–8in) apart. Named varieties must be divided, but the species can also be grown from seed sown as soon as it is ripe in July. Overwinter the seedlings in a greenhouse or frame. Pot up when the new leaves begin to show in the spring.

Feeding Apply a little general fertiliser as growth commences in the spring.

Problems No specific pest or disease problems are known for this plant.

FLOWERING

Season Flowers appear in the spring and early summer, generally before the leaves. They last well and the display is prolonged by the pretty, silky seedheads.

Cutting Flowers are unsuitable for cutting, but the seedheads add to an attractive display.

AFTER FLOWERING

Requirements Plants should be left alone until the seedheads have faded or fallen. Cut off spent stems, and as the plant dies trim off the foliage.

RANUNCULUS
Buttercup

A STRONG, vivid display of ranunculus showing how they can enliven a border. By mixing two or three different varieties you will certainly get extra impact. However, since some types of ranunculus can rapidly multiply and spread, you must take great care when selecting a particular variety.

FEATURES

EVERGREEN

HERBACEOUS

Buttercups basically divide into the invasive and the less-so. Take care which you chose for the border. The genus contains about 400 species of annuals, biennials and perennials, with a wide range of demands, which vary from free-draining alpine slopes to ponds. *R. ficaria*, lesser celndine, is a woodland type with early spring, yellow flowers that can become a weed. There are several cultivars; 'Brazen Hussy' has dark brown foliage and yellow flowers, while 'Salmon's White' is cream with a blue tint on the reverse. *R. aconitifolius* 'Flore Pleno', fair maids of France, likes full sun and has white, long-lasting flowers. And *R. flammula*, lesser spearwort, is a marginal aquatic for early summer with yellow flowers.

RANUNCULUS AT A GLANCE

A large genus of over 400 species with many annuals, biennials, and perennials, hardy to −15°C (5°F) for all kinds of garden.

		RECOMMENDED VARIETIES
JAN	/	
FEB	/	*Ranunculus aconitifolius*
MAR	sow	'Flore Pleno'
APR	transplant	R. calandrinioides
MAY	flowering	R. ficaria 'Brazen Hussy'
JUN	flowering	R. f. 'Picton's Double'
JULY	flowering	R. f. 'Salmon's White'
AUG	/	R. flammula
SEPT	/	R. gramineus
OCT	dvide	R. montanus 'Molten Gold'
NOV	/	
DEC	/	

CONDITIONS

Aspect It tolerates a wide range of conditions from medium to dappled shade, to full sun. When buying a ranunculus do carefully check its specific needs.

Site This too varies considerably from moist, rich soil, to fertile, free-draining ground, to gritty, fast-draining soil for the alpine types, to ponds and pond margins for the aquatics.

GROWING METHOD

Propagation Divide in the spring or autumn, or sow fresh, ripe seed in the autumn.

Feeding This depends entirely on the natural habitat and growing needs of the plant. Border perennials need reasonable applications of well-rotted manure in the spring, as new growth appears, while the woodland types need plenty of leafy compost dug in around the clumps.

Problems Slugs and snails are a particular nuisance; pick off or use chemical treatment.

FLOWERING

Season From late spring to mid-summer, depending on the chosen variety.

Cutting All ranunculus make excellent cut flowers, being especially useful in spring before the main flush of garden flowers.

AFTER FLOWERING

Requirements Cut back all spent stems.

RODGERSIA
Rodgersia

NO GARDEN IS COMPLETE without rodgersia. They can be grown apart from other plants, perhaps surrounded by gravel, highlighting the shapely, distinctive leaves, which on R. pinnata *grow 25cm (10in) long. Or grow them in a mixed border, where they add strength and structure.*

FEATURES

HERBACEOUS

A six-species genus with particularly interesting foliage, and flowers, ideal for the border or shady woodland garden. The three most commonly grown types are *R. aesculifolia, R. pinnata,* and *R. podophylla* (the last two having handsome, bronze new foliage). All form big, bold clumps in the right conditions. The first has crinkled leaves like those of a horse-chestnut, up to 25cm (10in) long, with tall panicles of creamy white flowers; height 2m (6½ft). *R. pinnata* 'Superba', 1.2m (4ft), has purple-bronze foliage and white, pink or red flowers. And *R. podophylla,* 1.5m (5ft), with creamy green flowers, also has horse-chestnut-type leaves, reddish in the autumn.

RODGERSIA AT A GLANCE

These tall, clump-forming perennials add structure to any damp-ish garden. Whitish summer flowers; hardy to –18ºC (0ºF).

		RECOMMENDED VARIETIES
JAN	/	
FEB	/	*Rodgersia aesculifolia*
MAR	sow	*R. pinnata*
APR	dvide	*R. p.* 'Elegans'
MAY	transplant	*R. p.* 'Superba'
JUN	/	*R. podophylla*
JULY	flowering	*R. sambucifolia*
AUG	flowering	
SEPT	/	
OCT	/	
NOV	/	
DEC	/	

CONDITIONS

Aspect   Rodgersia, from the mountaineous Far East, like full sun or partial shade. They thrive in both conditions.

Site   Grow in rich, damp ground; they grow by streams in the wild, and also in woodland settings.

GROWING METHOD

Propagation   Either divide, which is the easiest method, or grow from seed in the spring, raising the plants in a cold frame. Water the new young plants well, and do not let them dry out in prolonged, dry spells. They quickly wilt and lose energy, and their performance is badly affected.

Feeding   Add plenty of well-rotted manure or compost to the soil. The shadier the conditions, the less rich the soil need be.

Problems   Vine weevil grubs can demolish the roots of container-grown perennials. While slugs rarely attack the new emerging growth, when they do strike they can ruin a potentially impressive display with tall, astilbe-like flowers. Pick off any offenders or treat with a chemical.

FLOWERING

Season   Flowers appear in mid- and late summer, and in early summer in the case of *R. sambucifolia.*

Cutting   Rodgersia make good cut flowers, helping create an impressive display.

AFTER FLOWERING

Requirements   Cut the spent stems to the ground, and promptly remove all debris.

ROMNEYA COULTERI

Californian tree poppy

CRIMPED WHITE PETALS around a mass of golden stamens, making the matilija poppy as effective in close-up as in a group.

THE BLUE-GREEN FOLIAGE and splendid white flowers of the matilija poppy make an eye-catching display in the garden.

FEATURES

Also known as the matilija poppy, this lovely perennial is not always easy to accommodate. It is native to the canyons and dry riverbeds in parts of California where there is generally rain only in winter, and where summers are hot and dry. When conditions are suitable this plant can spread via underground roots. The large, white, summer flowers have beautiful crinkled petals that look like silk. Plants grow from 1–2m (3-6½ft) high, and the blue-green foliage is deeply cut and attractive. Place these perennials in groups among shrubs or mixed perennials. Most plants available are likely to be hybrids of the straight species and *R. coulteri* var. *trichocalyx*.

ROMNEYA AT A GLANCE

R. coulteri is a deciduous sub-shrub with grey-green leaves and highly attractive white summer flowers. Hardy to –18ºC (0ºF).

		COMPANION PLANTS
JAN	/	
FEB	/	
MAR	sow	Ceanothus
APR	division	Clematis
MAY	transplant	Delphinium
JUN	flowering	Helenium
JULY	flowering	Hemerocallis
AUG	flowering	Pelargonium
SEPT	/	Pennisetum
OCT	/	Philadelphus
NOV	/	
DEC	/	

CONDITIONS

Aspect Needs bright, full sun all day.
Site Needs well-drained, preferably sandy or gravelly loam; avoid thick, heavy, wet clay. They can be tricky and slow to establish, but thereafter thrive given the right conditions.

GROWING METHOD

Propagation Grows from seed sown in the spring, but it is easiest propagated from root cuttings or suckers growing away from the main plant in spring. Wait until plants are very well established before attempting to disturb the roots – something they do not react well to. Space plants approximately 40cm (16in) apart. Water regularly in the spring when the foliage is growing and buds are appearing; thereafter water occasionally in prolonged, dry spells.
Feeding Give a little complete plant food in early spring.
Problems Poor drainage can kill Californian tree poppies. Can become invasive.

FLOWERING

Season Right through the summer.
Cutting Like all poppies they make lovely cut flowers. Scald or burn the stems before arranging.

AFTER FLOWERING

Requirements Cut off spent flowers. As the plant flowers on new growth it is best to cut it down to the ground in winter. Protect the crown with straw or bracken in cold areas.

RUDBECKIA
Coneflower

THE DAISY-LIKE flower shape of the coneflower, a bright colour, and a central dark marking. It looks best in a bold group display.

A VALUABLE, forceful, late summer display from a mass planting of coneflowers, especially useful when many borders are starting to fade.

FEATURES

HERBACEOUS

The coneflower rewards a bright, sunny position with a bold display of daisy-like flowers. The genus consists of annuals, biennials and perennials, with some traditional garden favourites. *R. fulgida*, black-eyed Susan, grows 90 x 45cm (36 x 18in), producing yellow-orange flowers at the end of summer, into the autumn. 'Goldsturm' has bigger flowers but only grows two-thirds as tall. For a powerful, vigorous display at the back of the border, try *R. lacinata*. It has thin wiry stems, lemon-yellow flowers, and puts on a mid-summer to mid-autumn display that can reach 2.4m (8ft) high, while its spread is relatively contained, just 1m (3ft).

RUDBECKIA AT A GLANCE

A near 20-species genus with annuals, biennials and perennials, often with striking, yellowish flowers. Hardy to –18ºC (0ºF).

JAN	/	
FEB	/	
MAR	sow	
APR	divide	
MAY	transplant	
JUN	/	
JULY	flowering	
AUG	flowering	
SEPT	flowering	
OCT	flowering	
NOV	divide	
DEC	/	

RECOMMENDED VARIETIES

'Goldquelle'
'Herbstonne'
Rudbeckia fulgida var. *deamii*
R. f. var. *sullivantii*
  'Goldsturm'
R. laciniata
R. maxima

CONDITIONS

Aspect A bright, open sunny position is essential. Avoid shady areas. The plant's natural habitat is North American meadows and big, open woods.

Site Do not plant in over-dry, Mediterranean-type gardens. The soil must remain heavy, on the damp side. In the wild *R. fulgida* grows in marshy valleys.

GROWING METHOD

Propagation Either divide in the spring or autumn, or sow seeds in spring in a cold frame. Do not let the new young plants dry out.

Feeding Fertility must be quite high. Dig in large quantities of well-rotted manure and compost to poor soil.

Problems Slugs can be a major problem. Keep watch, and pick them off by hand or treat chemically. A potentially good flowering display can be quickly ruined if they take control.

FLOWERING

Season A long flowering season from the summer to late autumn.

Cutting Rudbeckia make good cut flowers, adding height and colour to any arrangement. They are especially useful having a dark coloured central disc (black, brown or green) in the centre of the flower.

AFTER FLOWERING

Requirements Cut back to the ground, though some stems can be left to provide interesting shapes over winter, especially when frosted.

SALVIA
Sage

SALVIA X SYLVESTRIS 'MAINACHT' ('MAY NIGHT') is a wonderful, clumpy perennial that sends up spires of rich blue flowers. It can be guaranteed to soften even the most rigid landscaped garden, flowering in early and mid-summer. 'Blauhugel' ('Blue Mound') is very similar.

FEATURES

SUMMER AUTUMN WINTER SPRING

HERBACEOUS

SUMMER AUTUMN WINTER SPRING

EVERGREEN

Salvias are a huge plant group of over 700 species, comprising shrubs, herbaceous perennials and annuals. Most people associate salvias with red or purple flowers but there are also species with cream, yellow, white, blue or pink flowers. Many have highly aromatic foliage with scents ranging from the delicious to the outright unpleasant: the foliage of pineapple sage, *S. elegans* (syn. *S. rutilans*) has a delicious perfume while the bog sage (*S. uliginosa*) smells rather unpleasant. Most salvias are extremely easy to grow and once established need little attention beyond occasional deep watering in hot weather and some cutting back after flowering. The tall salvias are ideal for the back of the border or for fillers between shrubs. There are many others of varying heights that are suitable as edging plants or for planting among annuals, bulbs and other perennials. *Salvia* x *sylvestris* 'Mainacht" ('May Night'), shown above, is an exceptionally good border perennial, but if it is unavailable there are plenty of fine alternatives, including 'Rose Queen'. Common sage, *S. officinalis*, is a highly popular salvia. It has grey, rather wrinkly foliage and flowers that are usually pale violet. The one problem is that in the right conditions it spreads like a weed. Coming from the Mediterranean it demands sharp drainage and dislikes a soaking wet summer.

Others

For spring–summer flowers in a range of colours, from cream to lilac and blue, try *S. sclarea*. It is perfectly hardy, and grows up to 90cm (3ft) high. *S. bulleyana* is equally easy, and grows about 40–90cm (16in–3ft) high. It has yellow flowers with a brownish lower lip appearing from the middle to the end of summer, and is also fully hardy, coming from western China. For an early summer–autumn flower show, use *S. forsskaolii* from the Black Sea coast. It grows 90cm (3ft) high, and bears white flowers with lips in violet, and faint yellow. Alternatively try *S.* x *superba*. It has violet flowers from mid-summer to autumn, and reaches the same height. For mild areas where you can grow half-hardy plants, there are plenty more salvias including *S. microphylla*, and the bog sage, *S. uliginosa*. The former has rich green leaves and magenta flowers at the end of summer–early autumn. Bog sage has bright blue flowers with a touch of white, and blooms from late summer to autumn. Both reach 90cm (3ft) high.

CONDITIONS

Aspect
Provide full sun, perhaps in a scree bed, and, in the case of half-hardy plants, a place against a south-facing wall.

Site
Any well-drained soil is suitable. Mulching with decayed manure in early spring improves the soil condition.

SALVIA SCLAREA *VAR.* TURKESTANICA *can be grown as a perennial or biennial. It produces wonderful pink stems of pinky-white flowers, and is perfectly hardy.*

THE ELECTRIC BLUE *Salvia transsylvanica contrasting with a Star Gazer lily.*

GROWING METHOD

Propagation   Salvias grow from seed that has been sown in the spring, or from cuttings which have been taken in late summer through to the autumn. Many species can also be propagated from rooted divisions of an established clump. Simply lift such a clump and you will find numerous pieces with both roots and shoots. The divisions are best taken in the spring months. Set each division approximately 25cm (10in) apart. Needs regular watering to establish. Once established, plants can be drought tolerant.

Feeding   A complete plant food or pelleted poultry manure can be applied in the spring, in poor soil, as the new growth commences. However, note that too much fertiliser will be counter-productive, merely resulting in all foliage and very few flowers.

Problems   The worst problems tend to occur when you provide a certain species with the wrong conditions. Carefully check the notes invariably supplied with plants when buying from a garden centre, or specialist nursery. As a general rule, avoid damp ground and any shady areas.

FLOWERING

Season   Many salvias have a very long flowering period, extending into the autumn before being cut down by the frosts.

Cutting   None of the salvias mentioned makes a particularly good cut flower, but their long, dependable flowering season does make them a great asset in any part of the garden.

AFTER FLOWERING

Requirements   Borderline, half-hardy species will need plenty of protection in cold areas over winter. Provide a thick, protective layer of straw or bracken, held in place with sticks. As a precaution against any losses, keep a stock of new, young plants. The tender salvias must be kept indoors in winter, in a frost-free place. Plants can be tip pruned after each flowering flush to promote further blooming. In late autumn plants can be cut back just above ground level. If you do not want to lift and divide a clump you can wait until new growth starts in the spring, and simply divide any growth that is becoming too crowded. A number of perennial salvias are extremely vigorous, but they can be kept in control by pulling out the new plants or running roots when they are getting invasive.

SALVIA AT A GLANCE

A large genus with fine perennials. The colour range is mainly blue. Hardy plants to −18°C (0°F); half-hardy −5°C (23°F).

		RECOMMENDED VARIETIES
JAN	/	
FEB	/	*Salvia argentea*
MAR	sow	*S. bulleyana*
APR	divide	*S. forsskaolii*
MAY	transplant	*S. involucrata* (half-hardy)
JUN	flowering	*S. microphylla* (half-hardy)
JULY	flowering	*S. patens* (half-hardy)
AUG	flowering	*S. sclarea*
SEPT	flowering	*S. x superba*
OCT	flowering	*S. uliginosa* (half-hardy)
NOV	/	
DEC	/	

SCABIOSA
Scabious

SCABIOSA CAUCASICA 'CLIVE GREAVES' is a wonderful lavender-blue, looking especially impressive when planted in clusters.

SCABIOUS ARE VERSATILE PLANTS. They make a wonderful addition to most gardens, whether schematic or cottagey.

FEATURES

Scabious is a vital ingredient of cottage-style, flowery gardens, rock gardens and mixed borders. From hot, dry, stoney sites, mainly in the Mediterranean, it provides pale hues in blue, pink, yellow or white. The flowers are held above long, thin stems, many attracting bees and butterflies. Heights generally range from 30–90cm (12–36in). There are plenty of interesting choices, and top of the list are the dwarf forms 'Butterfly Blue' and 'Pink Mist', both relatively new, and proving extremely popular. On the plus side they flower for six months; the down side is they are short lived. Take cuttings to maintain the display.

SCABIOSA AT A GLANCE

A genus of annuals, biennials and perennials, providing abundant soft colours. Good for romantic displays. Hardy to –18°C (0°F).

JAN	/	RECOMMENDED VARIETIES
FEB	/	
MAR	sow	*Scabiosa caucasica*
APR	divide	'Clive Greaves'
MAY	transplant	*S. c.* 'Miss Willmott'
JUN	flowering	'Chile Black'
JULY	flowering	*S. columbaria* var. *ochroleuca*
AUG	flowering	*S. lucida*
SEPT	flowering	'Pink Mist'
OCT	sow	
NOV	/	
DEC	/	

CONDITIONS

Aspect Full sun is essential.
Site Dryish, free-draining soil is important so that the roots are not plunged in soaking wet ground over the winter months. The soil must also veer from the neutral towards the slightly alkaline.

GROWING METHOD

Propagation Scabious is not long-living, and begins to lose its vigour and impact after three years. It is therefore vital to replenish the garden with either spring divisions, or to sow fresh, ripe seed in pots in a cold frame to maintain a good supply.
Feeding Do not over-feed the soil which will be counter-productive, producing leaf growth at the expense of flowers. Very poor soils, though, might need some additions of compost in the early spring.
Problems Spray at the first sign of powdery mildew.

FLOWERING

Season The flowers appear right through the summer, in some cases not until mid-summer, often into early autumn.
Cutting Scabious make excellent sprays of cut flowers, and are indispensable for indoor arrangements, either adding to flowery schemes or softening more rigid, structural ones.

AFTER FLOWERING

Requirements Cut all spent stems down to the ground.

SEDUM SPECTABILE
Ice plant

DENSE FLOWERHEADS of Sedum spectabile 'Brilliant' provide a rich source of nectar, attracting butterflies and other insects.

BILLOWING HEADS of sedum add colour to the autumn garden. Here they edge a mixed border, with white beard tongue behind.

FEATURES

One of over 600 species of succulent sedums, this is unusual because it is frequently used in perennial plantings where many succulents look out of place. It has fleshy, soft green leaves on stems that can reach 60cm (24in) high. Similar varieties are available with purple and variegated leaves. Since the new growth appears at the base of older stems, dividing plants is easy. The large heads of flowers are a soft mauve-pink in the species, but there are cultivars with colours ranging from bright hot pinks to rosy red, and the brick red of 'Herbstfreude' ('Autumn Joy'). The plants flower from late summer into autumn. This is an easy-care plant that accepts a wide range of conditions.

SEDUM AT A GLANCE

S. spectabile is a clump-forming, late season perennial with pink flowers. Many excellent forms. Hardy to −15°C (5°F).

JAN	/	
FEB	/	
MAR	/	
APR	divide	
MAY	/	
JUN	/	
JULY	/	
AUG	flowering	
SEPT	flowering	
OCT	divide	
NOV	sow	
DEC	/	

RECOMMENDED VARIETIES

Sedum alboroseum
 'Mediovariegatum'
S. cauticola
'Herbstfreude' ('Autumn Joy')
'Ruby Glow'
S. spectabile 'Brilliant'
S. telephium maximum
 'Atropurpureum'

CONDITIONS

Aspect Prefers full sun, but tolerates some light shade for part of the day.
Site While it can grow in a sandy, well-drained soil, it will tolerate a heavier soil which gives it an advantage over other sedums.

GROWING METHOD

Propagation Clumps of plants are easily pulled, or sliced, apart with a spade in the spring or late autumn. The divisions are best replanted at approximately 15–20cm (6–8in) intervals. Division gives very high success rates. It is also possible to propagate sedum by striking from stem cuttings. Water regularly to establish new young plants.
Feeding Slow-release fertiliser can be applied in the spring, as new growth commences. Avoid overfeeding because this may result in plenty of sappy leaf growth at the expense of a display of flowers.
Problems Plants in containers may rot at the base if overwatered. Vine weevil grubs may also devour both bases and roots with devastating effect.

FLOWERING

Season The late, highly rewarding display occurs at the end of summer, running through autumn.
Cutting A long-lasting cut flower.

AFTER FLOWERING

Requirements Leave the skeletal flowerheads over winter to provide attractive, burnished tints.

SISYRINCHIUM

Sisyrinchrium

SISYRINCHIUM IDAHOENSE 'ALBUM' *is a clump-forming white flower that at 12cm (5in) high is ideal for edging borders.*

SISYRINCHIUM MACROCARPON *is 75cm (30in) tall, has eye-catching vertical foliage, and gentle yellow flowers in early summer.*

FEATURES

SUMMER AUTUMN WINTER SPRING

EVERGREEN

This is a star plant for the border, with spires of pale yellow flowers over summer, 90cm (36in) high, and iris-like, strap-shape foliage. The only problem is that it can self-seed too much for the liking of some, though with vigilance the seedlings are easily removed. The genus also offers blue, mauve and white flowers. *S. idahoense* is a lovely violet-blue, with a yellow throat, growing 30cm (12in) high, while *S. graminoides* is slightly taller at 20in (50cm), with a deeper blue flower, though it does self-seed more prolifically. For a dwarfish, low-growing white try 'Pole Star', good for the rock garden where it can best be seen and appreciated. It grows just 2.5 x 6cm (1 x 2½in), and is perfectly hardy.

SISYRINCHIUM AT A GLANCE

S. striatum is an evergreen perennial with spires of pale yellow flowers, and long, stiff, pointed leaves. Hardy to −15ºC (5ºF).

		RECOMMENDED VARIETIES
JAN	/	*Sisyrinchium angustifolium*
FEB	/	'Biscutella'
MAR	sow	'Californian Skies'
APR	transplant	*S. californicum*
MAY	/	'E. K. Balls'
JUN	flowering	*S. idahoense*
JULY	flowering	*S. macrocarpon*
AUG	/	'Quaint and Queer'
SEPT	divide	*S. striatum* 'Aunt May'
OCT	/	
NOV	/	
DEC	/	

CONDITIONS

Aspect Full sun is required, well away from the shade.
Site Relatively poor soil is quite adequate, but free-draining ground is essential. Do not let the plants stand out in damp, wet soil over the winter months.

GROWING METHOD

Propagation Divide in late summer to guarantee a supply of vigorous plants since mature ones become quite lack-lustre after three years. Alternatively, sow seed in the spring. To prevent any established plants from self-seeding, cut off the flowers the moment they begin to fade.

Feeding Some enriching with well-rotted manure or compost will provide a boost to poor areas of ground. High levels of fertility, however, are not necessary.

Problems Generally trouble free.

FLOWERING

Season Flowers in early and mid-summer.
Cutting They make unusual, striking cut flowers, adding smart verticals to any arrangement, forming the basic structure. Use both flowering stems and foliage.

AFTER FLOWERING

Requirements Cut back the flowering stems to the ground, either promptly to prevent large-scale self-seeding, or later to increase numbers, especially when established plants are past their best.

SOLIDAGO
Golden rod

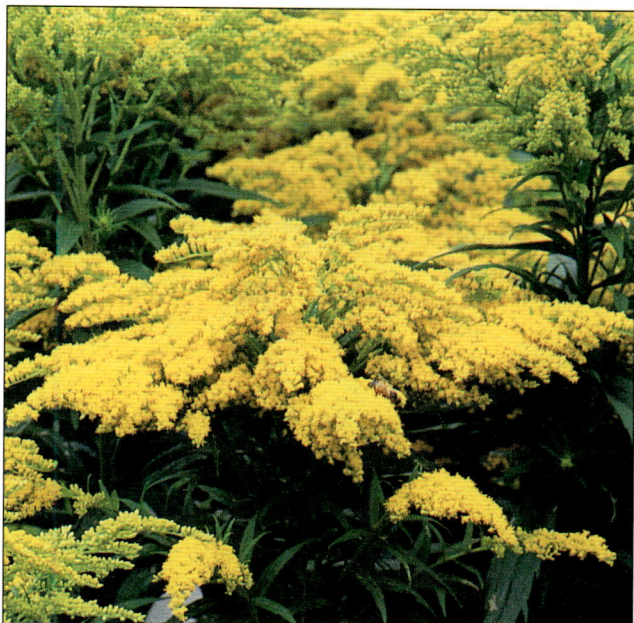

THE HIGHLY DISTINCTIVE *sight of golden rod. A bright spray of yellow flowers, and the long, thin, dark green leaves.*

A PERFECT EXAMPLE OF HOW *an invasive plant, such as golden rod, can be reigned in and controlled by hard landscaping.*

FEATURES

SUMMER AUTUMN WINTER SPRING

HERBACEOUS

Golden rod forms large colonies of sometimes quite tall yellow plants, reaching 1.8m (6ft) high. The small flowers in themselves are nothing special, but they appear in such profusion that they actually make quite an impact. There are plenty of varieties to choose from. The key differences are more to do with height than colour. 'Crown of Rays' grows 60cm (24in) high, and as its name suggests has bright yellow flowers. 'Goldenmosa' is almost as bright and grows slightly taller, and also has yellow-green foliage. But if you need a golden rod for the back of the border, especially one where the soil is quite poor, the best choice is 'Golden Wings'. It can reach 1.8m (6ft) high,

topping smaller plants with its late summer and early autumn show. The best choice of golden rod for growing at the front of the border is the 20cm (8in) high 'Queenie' or *S. virgaurea minuta*.

CONDITIONS

Aspect   Grow in full sun in the border. Avoid borders that are in the shade.
Site   Free-draining soil, preferably quite sandy or gritty, is ideal.

GROWING METHOD

Propagation Golden rod self-seeds but to be sure of getting new plants that are true to type, spring or autumn division invariably give successful results.
Feeding   High soil fertility is not in any way essential. Very poor ground can be improved, though, in the spring by digging in some quantities of well-rotted manure.
Problems   Powdery mildew can strike quite severely; treat with a fungicide at the first sight of an attack, repeat sprayings being necessary to control major outbreaks.

FLOWERING

Season   Generally mid- to late summer, though sometimes slightly before and after.
Cutting   Not the best cut flowers, there are better alternatives, but they effectively bulk up any arrangement.

AFTER FLOWERING

Requirements Cut back spent flower stems.

SOLIDAGO AT A GLANCE

Varieties of golden rod create mainly big, bold, clumps of bright yellow flowers. Can be invasive. Hardy to −18°C (0°F).

		RECOMMENDED VARIETIES
JAN	/	*Solidago cutleri*
FEB	/	*S. flexicaulis* 'Variegata'
MAR	/	'Golden Baby'
APR	divide	'Goldenmosa'
MAY	transplant	'Queenie'
JUN	/	*S. virgaurea minuta*
JULY	flowering	
AUG	flowering	
SEPT	/	
OCT	/	
NOV	/	
DEC	/	

STACHYS BYZANTINA
Lamb's ears

SINCE LAMB'S EARS, or lamb's tails, needs good drainage, grow it in an attractive container if your soil is relentlessly heavy and damp.

MORE TRADITIONAL is this planting, where lamb's ears edge a garden bed. The plants will multiply rapidly given the right situation.

FEATURES

HERBACEOUS

Lamb's ears is a low-growing, evergreen perennial most often used as an edging plant. It could also be used to edge rose beds, but wherever it is planted it must have excellent drainage and full exposure to the sun. The leaves are densely covered with hairs, giving them a white, or pale grey, woolly appearance, hence its common name. It does produce pink-purple flowers on spikes that stand above the foliage, but they are not especially attractive; it is grown for its foliage, not the flowers (*S. macrantha* 'Robusta, and *S. officinalis* are the exception). 'Cotton Boll' has woolly flowers good for dried flower arrangements if they are cut when fully open. Plants grow 15–20cm (6–8in) high, but spread a good distance.

STACHYS AT A GLANCE

S. byzantina is a valuable garden plant, noted for its front-of-the-border colour and soft, silky foliage. Hardy to –18°C (0°F).

		RECOMMENDED VARIETIES
JAN	/	
FEB	/	*S. coccinea*
MAR	sow	*Stachys byzantina* 'Big Ears'
APR	divide	*S. b.* 'Cotton Boll'
MAY	transplant	*S. b.* 'Primrose Heron'
JUN	flowering	*S. macrantha*
JULY	flowering	*S. m.* 'Robusta'
AUG	flowering	*S. officinalis*
SEPT	flowering	
OCT	divide	
NOV	/	
DEC	/	

CONDITIONS

Aspect Full sun is essential all day for the plants to thrive and perform well.

Site Needs very fast draining soil. It grows well in poor, sandy or gravelly soil. Avoid thick, wet heavy clay at all costs.

GROWING METHOD

Propagation Grows readily from cuttings that are taken in the spring or autumn. The new divisions must be planted out about 20cm (8in) apart. Water new plants regularly. Once they are established, they need only be watered very occasionally.

Feeding Grows without supplementary fertiliser, but a little complete plant food can be applied in the early spring.

Problems There are no specific problems but container plants will quickly fail if they are overwatered, and border plants rot if they are waterlogged.

FLOWERING

Season Flowers are produced in the summer, sometimes into autumn, but the tactile grey foliage is by far the chief attraction.

Cutting Use the foliage in an arrangement; the flower spikes can be cut and dried for later use.

AFTER FLOWERING

Requirements Cut spent flower stems right at the base. Trailing growth can be shortened back at any time, but plants may need to be cut back hard in the early spring.

STOKESIA LAEVIS

Stokes' aster

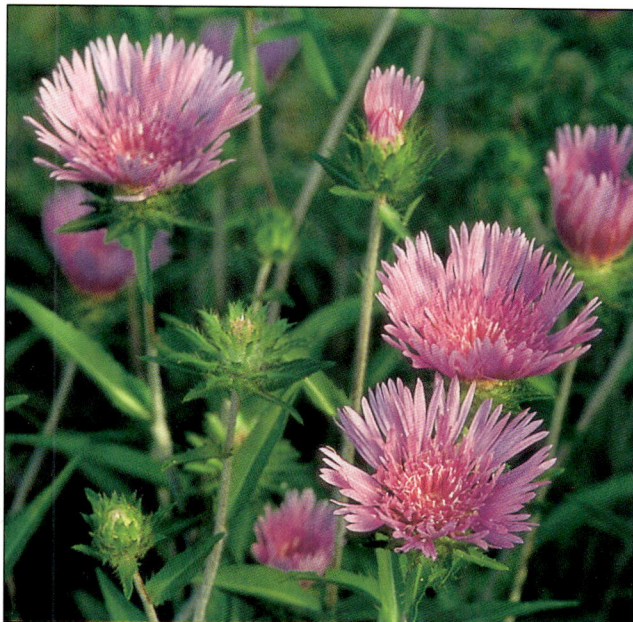

THE FLOWERING HEADS of Stokes' aster are quite complex, made up of many 'petals' (more properly bracts or ray florets).

IT IS HARD to understand why the pretty Stokes' aster should go out of fashion but it is certainly grown less often than before.

FEATURES

HERBACEOUS

Stokes' aster is an easy to grow plant that provides great decorative value throughout its long flowering period from mid-summer to early autumn. It makes excellent cut flowers, too. Flower stems 30–50cm (12–20in) high rise from a cluster of dark green basal leaves. Although this plant is completely herbaceous in cold areas, the basal growth remains evergreen in mild winters. Flowers are reminiscent of large cornflowers or asters, and come in shades of blue, white and mauve. This plant can look outstanding in mass plantings but is equally at home in a mixed border, or when grown in wooden tubs or pots.

STOKESIA AT A GLANCE

S. laevis is an evergreen, perennial, sprawling plant with large, purple, flat, late summer flowers. Hardy to –15°C (5°F).

		Companion Plants
Jan	/	
Feb	sow	Aster
Mar	divide	Box
Apr	transplant	Dahlia
May	transplant	Fuchsia
Jun	/	Miscanthus
July	/	Penstemon
Aug	flowering	Potentilla
Sept	flowering	Stipa
Oct	flowering	
Nov	divide	
Dec	/	

CONDITIONS

Aspect While it prefers full sun, it just about tolerates dappled shade. Provide a shelter to protect from strong winds.

Site Needs well-drained soil enriched with compost or manure.

GROWING METHOD

Propagation Divide established clumps in spring or autumn, replanting divisions about 25cm (10in) apart. The plant can also be grown from root cuttings taken in early spring, and from autumn seed. Tolerates dry periods, but looks best if given an occasional deep watering in prolonged, dry spells. Provide young plants with twiggy support.

Feeding Apply some complete plant food in the spring.

Problems Poorly drained, heavy soils induce root or crown rot, which kills plants.

FLOWERING

Season The long flowering period is from late summer into the autumn.

Cutting Cut flowers regularly for the vase. This both gives a good ornamental display and prolongs the garden show, inducing plenty of new flower buds.

AFTER FLOWERING

Requirements Prune all spent flower stems. As the growth dies back, promptly clear away all the dead foliage.

THALICTRUM
Meadow rue

THE FLUFFY PINK FLOWERS of meadow rue do not last long, but the pretty foliage persists well until the autumn.

FINER FOLIAGE, smaller starry flowers and very full growth are features of the related Thalictrum delavayi *and its cultivars.*

FEATURES

Thalictrum aquilegiifolium is easy and quick to grow, a herbaceous perennial reaching about 1m (42in) high. The rather fern-like, blue-green foliage is attractively lobed, and the flowers are mauve-pink in dense, fluffy heads. While the floral display does not last long, the foliage adds months of charm. Meadow rue can be planted in mixed borders or in light shade under trees. There are a number of cultivars, including a white form and one with violet blooms. Also try *T. delavayi* (syn. *T. dipterocarpum*) and its cultivars 'Album' and 'Hewitt's Double'. This has finer foliage and the pink-mauve flowers are star shaped.

THALICTRUM AT A GLANCE

T. aquilegiifolium is a clump-forming, rhizomatous perennial with lovely sprays of purple flowers. Hardy to −18°C (5°F).

		RECOMMENDED VARIETIES
JAN	/	*Thalictrum aquilegiifolium*
FEB	/	var. *album*
MAR	divide	*T. a.* 'Thundercloud'
APR	transplant	*T. delavayi*
MAY	/	*T. flavum* subsp. *glaucum*
JUN	flowering	*T. kiusianum*
JULY	flowering	*T. minus*
AUG	/	*T. rochebruneanum*
SEPT	/	
OCT	sow	
NOV	/	
DEC	/	

CONDITIONS

Aspect   Grow in either light shade, or in a border with morning sun followed by plenty of afternoon shade.

Soil   Likes well-drained soil that has been enriched with organic matter.

GROWING METHOD

Propagation   Grows from seed sown in the spring or autumn, or by divisions of a clump made in spring. Plant the new divisions about 25–30cm (10–12in) apart. Do not let the young plants dry out, giving regular, deep watering through a dry spring and summer.

Feeding   As growth begins in the spring apply complete plant food, and mulch around the plants with well-decayed manure or compost.

Problems   No specific pest or disease problems are known to attack this plant. Generally trouble free. Note that growth begins late in spring, so avoid damaging new growth while weeding.

FLOWERING

Season   Flowers appear during early summer, depending on the temperatures.

Cutting   Both the foliage and flowers can be cut for the vase.

AFTER FLOWERING

Requirements Cut off any spent flower stems unless you want to save seed. When the plants die down in the autumn, cut off the foliage at ground level.

TIARELLA
Foam flower

THE FOAM FLOWER produces both a fine early summer flower display, and often burnt-red coloured autumn foliage.

GIVEN A FREE RUN, Tiarella polyphylla produces a large, spreading clump with wonderful spires of white flowers.

FEATURES

HERBACEOUS

Tiarella trifoliata is a North American clump-forming rhizomatous perennial, making excellent groundcover in light shade. From late spring to mid-summer it produces light airy sprays of white flowers, on 30cm (12in) long panicles, held above the foliage. A more invasive plant is *T. cordifolia,* foam flower, from east North America where it grows in mountainside woods, forming extensive colonies, remorselessly spreading by underground stolons. *T. wherryi,* also from North America, is more compact and less invasive – the better choice for a smaller, shady area. Its natural habitat is shady ravines and rocky woods. The white flowers are tinged pink. 'Bronze Beauty' is a popular choice, benefiting from contrasting white flowers and bronze-red foliage.

CONDITIONS

Aspect   Thrives in both dappled and darkish shade, which is its natural habitat.

Site   It tolerates a wide range of soils, but naturally prefers rich, fertile ground, damp but definitely not boggy.

GROWING METHOD

Propagation   Division is the simplest method, though ripe seed can also be sown. Sow in pots in the autumn in a cold frame, and keep young plants well watered. Do not let them dry out.

Feeding   The ground needs to be quite rich. Fork in leafmould and compost in the early spring, and again in the autumn, between plants.

Problems   Slugs can strike but given the situation, out of the way in the shade, and the plant's vigour, it is rarely a major problem. Treat with slug pellets if matters get out of hand.

HARVESTING

Season   A profusion of white flowers appear from late spring to mid-summer.

Cutting   There are better choices for airy white sprays in the summer, but nonetheless they make decent cut flowers.

AFTER FLOWERING

Requirements   Cut back to the ground.

TIARELLA AT A GLANCE

T. trifoliata is a North American, white perennial, ideal for spreading quickly through shady sites. Hardy to -15°C (5°F).

		RECOMMENDED VARIETIES
JAN	/	
FEB	/	*Tiarella cordifolia*
MAR	sow	'Elizabeth Oliver'
APR	divide	*T. polyphylla*
MAY	flowering	*T. p.* pink
JUN	flowering	*T. wherryi*
JULY	flowering	*T. w.* 'Bronze Beauty'
AUG	/	
SEPT	sow	
OCT	/	
NOV	/	
DEC	/	

TRADESCANTIA

Tradescantia / spiderwort

SPIDERWORT FLOWERS look like small purple irises but each lasts only a day. The surrounding buds are waiting their turn to open.

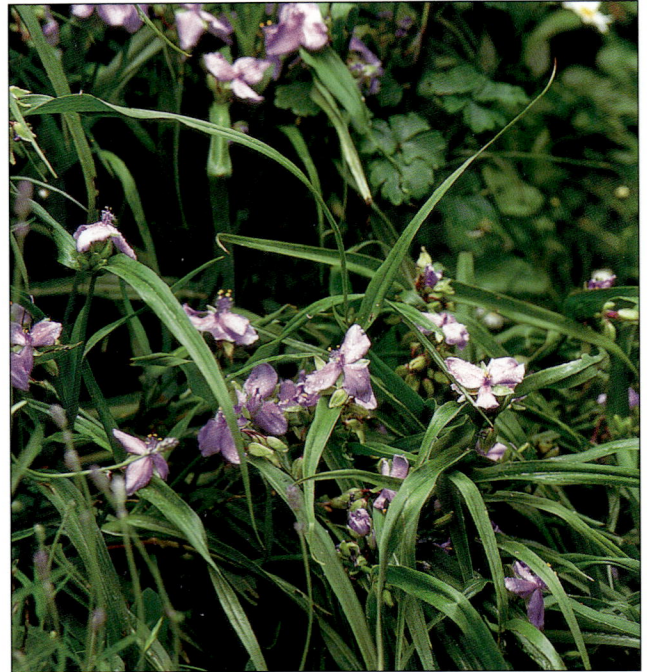

DENSE PLANTINGS of spiderwort produce plenty of flowers that thrive in filtered sunlight, ideal for a mixed or herbaceous border.

FEATURES

HERBACEOUS

This North American herbaceous perennial is a spreading plant with tapering, strap-like leaves and showy, triangular flowers in rich purple, rose-pink or white. The flowers generally last only one day but they appear in succession over a long period. There are several named cultivars available. Spiderwort grows from 30–60cm (12–24in) high, and is multi-stemmed. It is easy to grow in the right conditions and can make a tall groundcover in filtered sunlight under trees. In a mild winter it may not die down completely.

TRADESCANTIA AT A GLANCE

T. virginiana is a purple, repeat flowerer in a genus of largely tender indoor plants. Ideal for the border. Hardy to –15°C (5°F).

		RECOMMENDED VARIETIES
JAN	/	
FEB	/	*Tradescantia* x *andersoniana*
MAR	divide	'Bilberry Ice'
APR	/	*T.* x *a.* 'Isis'
MAY	/	*T.* x *a.* 'Osprey'
JUN	flowering	*T.* x *a.* 'Purple Dome'
JULY	flowering	*T.* x *a.* 'Red Cloud'
AUG	flowering	*T.* x *a.* 'Zwanenburg Blue'
SEPT	flowering	
OCT	divide	
NOV	divide	
DEC	/	

CONDITIONS

Aspect   It requires full sun or partial shade.
Site   It grows best in soil that is well drained, but is also heavily enriched with plenty of decayed, organic matter.

GROWING METHOD

Propagation   Clumps can be lifted and divided in the spring and autumn. The species can be grown from seed sown in autumn. It is occasionally self-sown. New plantings should be approximately 30–45cm (12–18in) apart, depending on how rapidly you need cover. Needs regular watering during a prolonged, dry growing period.
Feeding   Apply a complete plant food, as growth starts in the spring.
Problems   No specific problems are known.

FLOWERING

Season   The long succession of flowers starts in early summer and continues through to mid-autumn.
Cutting   The buds continue to open when cut.

AFTER FLOWERING

Requirements   Growth starts to yellow and die back after flowering. Clean away dead foliage, and tidy up for the winter.

TRILLIUM
Wake robin

THE WAKE ROBIN is the perfect plant for a moist shady area, whether it be light or deep shade. The plants are quickly identified by having three leaves, three calyces and three petals.

FEATURES

HERBACEOUS

Trilliums are deciduous perennials which make excellent groundcover in partial or full shade, with spring and early summer flowers. The colour range includes white, maroon, pink, yellow, bronze-green, and red-purple. *T. grandiflorum,* the North American wake robin, has 7.5cm (3in) long white flowers and veined petals. It is long-lived and easy to grow, requiring little attention. *T. sessile* 'Rubrum' has claret petals and attractively mottled foliage. Several clones bear this name and there is little to choose between them. At the front of a shady, slightly acidic border try *T. rivale.* It grows 12cm (6in) high and wide, has pointed ovate petals, white or pale pink, with purple speckling towards the base. *T. luteum* has scented yellowish flowers and mottled, pale and dark leaves. It grows 40cm (16in) high, spreading by almost the same amount.

CONDITIONS

Aspect	Mottled or deep shade is required. Avoid open areas with full sun.
Site	The soil should be the acid side of neutral, though in fact some trilliums will tolerate low levels of alkalinity.

GROWING METHOD

Propagation	Preferably divide the rhizomes when dormant, ensuring each section has one strong growing point. Note that they are slow to establish, though. It is quite possible to sow ripe, late summer seed in a cold frame, but the 5–7 years to flower is prohibitively long.
Feeding	The soil needs to be rich with plenty of well-rotted leafmould and compost, being damp and free draining. Where necessary provide a thick mulch every spring and autumn.
Problems	Both slugs and snails feed on the tender new foliage. Pick off by hand when this becomes a problem, or use a chemical treatment.

FLOWERING

Season	The flowers appear in spring and summer.
Cutting	They make attractive cut flowers, especially *T. grandiflorum* with its near diamond-shape white flowers.

AFTER FLOWERING

Requirements Cut spent stems to the ground.

TRILLIUM AT A GLANCE

A 30-species genus with rhizomatous perennials, excellent for flowering ground cover in shade. Hardy to −15°C (5°F).

Month		RECOMMENDED VARIETIES
JAN	/	*Trillium cernuum*
FEB	/	*T. chloropetalum*
MAR	/	*T. cuneatum*
APR	transplant	*T. erectum*
MAY	flowering	*T. grandiflorum*
JUN	flowering	*T. g. flore-pleno*
JULY	/	*T. luteum*
AUG	/	*T. rivale*
SEPT	sow	*T. viride*
OCT	divide	
NOV	/	
DEC	/	

VERBASCUM
Mullein

MULLEINS ARE FAMED for their striking shape and their bright flowers, but as seen here they can blend with the gentlest design.

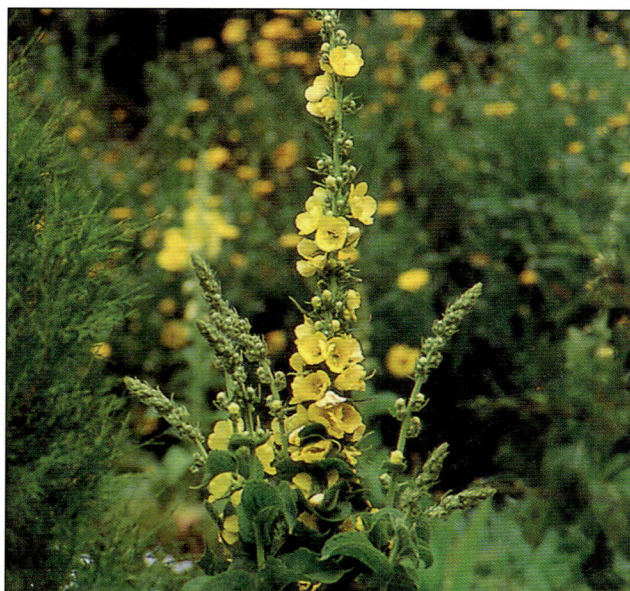

MULLEINS HAVE few equals as accent plants as they are tough and adaptable, capable of tolerating many climates and conditions.

FEATURES

EVERGREEN

HERBACEOUS

Not all mulleins are reliably perennial, some being best treated as biennials and replaced after two years. However, most are easy to raise. They are grown for their large rosettes of foliage, often silver or grey, from which emerges a tall, striking spike of flowers up to 1.8m (6ft) high. They make eye-catching accent plants in any sunny part of the garden. The various species and their cultivars have flowers in a range of colours, including white and gentler shades of yellow, pink and purple. The common mullein, *V. thapsus*, also known as Aaron's rod, freely self-seeds. Mullein has a long folk history, first as a candle, then as a medical treatment.

VERBASCUM AT A GLANCE

A 360-species genus, famed for its dramatic, coloured spires in summer. Heights 30cm–1.8m (12in–6ft). Hardy to –15°C (5°F).

		RECOMMENDED VARIETIES
JAN	/	*Verbascum bombyciferum*
FEB	/	*V. chaixii* 'Album'
MAR	/	*V. c.* 'Cotswold Beauty'
APR	sow	*V. c.* 'Gainsborough'
MAY	transplant	*V. dumulosum*
JUN	flowering	'Golden Wings'
JULY	flowering	'Helen Johnson'
AUG	flowering	'Letitia'
SEPT	sow	*V. phoeniceum*
OCT	/	
NOV	/	
DEC	/	

CONDITIONS

Aspect   Grows best in full sun all day.
Site   Grows in any kind of well-drained soil, even poor and alkaline ones.

GROWING METHOD

Propagation   Grows from seed sown as soon as it is ripe, or from root cuttings taken in late autumn or winter. The seed forms on the spike after the flowers have fallen, and is ripe when it has changed colour, becoming brown or black. Sow in pots in a cold frame in either the spring or autumn. Plants of the larger mullein species need to be planted out approximately 1m (39in) apart.

Feeding   Apply a complete plant food in early spring, as new growth commences.

Problems   No specific problems are known.

FLOWERING

Season   Mullein flowers right through the summer, but its amazing spire of a stem remains a big architectural feature long after the flowers have finished.

Cutting   A nipped off section of the flowering spire considerably adds to a formal, architectural display.

AFTER FLOWERING

Requirements   Cut off the spent flower spike unless you want seed to set.

VIOLA ODORATA
English violet

DESPITE *the range of cultivars available, the violet species is still a big favourite.*

VIOLETS PROVIDE *great groundcover under deciduous trees or in other shaded, sheltered spots. They do, however, need decent levels of sun to put on a good flowering display.*

FEATURES

EVERGREEN

Violets have been in cultivation since ancient times, and were highly valued by the ancient Greeks. In Victorian times an enormous number of varieties was grown, including a wide range of the double Parma violets. The violet's sweet fragrance and elegant flowers make them big favourites with gardeners and florists alike. The plants have a creeping habit, spreading up to 30cm (12in), and are rarely more than 15–20cm (6–8in) high. There are cultivars with single or double flowers in purple, pink, white or bicolours, but the deep purple is probably the best loved. There are other violet species to grow in the garden, from the summer-flowering V. *cornuta,* fine under hybrid tea roses, to the spring/summer V. *sororia,* and its form 'Freckles'.

VIOLA AT A GLANCE

V. *odorata* is a rhizomatous, semi-evergreen perennial with blue or white flowers. Good self-seeder. Hardy to −18°C (0°F).

		RECOMMENDED VARIETIES
JAN	/	
FEB	/	*Viola cornuta*
MAR	flowering	V. *c.* Alba Group
APR	flowering	V. *c.* Lilacina Group
MAY	flowering	V. *c.* 'Minor'
JUN	/	V. *odorata* 'Alba'
JULY	/	V. *o.* 'Rosea'
AUG	/	V. *sororia* 'Freckles'
SEPT	divide	V. *s.* 'Priceana'
OCT	/	
NOV	/	
DEC	/	

CONDITIONS

Aspect   It needs either shade, or light dappled sunlight.
Site   It needs well-drained, moisture-retentive soil, heavily enriched with organic matter for the best results.

GROWING METHOD

Propagation   Clumps can be lifted and divided, or runners can be dug up and replanted every couple of years, in the the spring or autumn. Set out at 20cm (8in) spacings, with the plant crowns kept just above soil level. Violets self-seed, too. Keep young plants well watered during the first growing season.
Feeding   Apply complete plant food in spring after flowering ceases.
Problems   Slugs and snails can be a major nuisance, devouring tasty new growth. Pick off by hand, or treat chemically.

FLOWERING

Season   Violets flower from late winter into early spring.
Cutting   Scalding the stems of cut violets before arranging them will certainly increase their vase life.

AFTER FLOWERING

Requirements   No special treatment is needed, but excess runners can be removed during the growing season if they are invasive. This has the added benefit of channelling vigour back to the main crown.

PLANT NAME	SPRING			SUMMER			AUTUMN			WINTER		
	EARLY	MID	LATE	EARLY	MID	LATE	EARLY	MID	LATE	EARLY	MID	LATE
Acanthus mollis				✿	✿							
Achillea				✿	✿	✿	✿					
Agapanthus					✿	✿	✿					
Alchemilla mollis				✿	✿	✿	✿					
Alstroemeria					✿	✿	✿					
Anemone x hybrida						✿	✿					
Aquilegia			✿	✿								
Armeria maritima				✿	✿	✿						
Aster					✿		✿	✿				
Astilbe hybrids			✿	✿	✿	✿	✿					
Astrantia major				✿								
Aurinia saxatilis			✿	✿								
Bergenia	✿	✿	✿									✿
Campanula			✿	✿	✿	✿	✿					
Centranthus ruber				✿	✿	✿	✿					
Chrysanthemum					✿		✿					
Convallaria			✿									
Coreopsis				✿	✿	✿	✿					
Corydalis				✿	✿	✿						
Cynara cardunculus				✿	✿	✿	✿					
Delphinium				✿	✿	✿						
Dianthus caryophyllus				✿	✿	✿						
Dianthus cultivars				✿	✿	✿						
Diascia			✿	✿	✿	✿	✿					
Dicentra spectabilis				✿	✿							
Digitalis				✿	✿							
Echinacea purpurea					✿	✿	✿					
Echinops					✿	✿	✿					
Epimedium			✿									
Eryngium				✿	✿	✿	✿					
Euphorbia			✿	✿	✿	✿	✿					
Geranium				✿	✿	✿	✿					
Geum chiloense			✿	✿								
Gunnera manicata					✿							
Gypsophila paniculata					✿	✿						
Helenium autumnale					✿	✿	✿					
Helleborus	✿											✿
Hemerocallis				✿	✿	✿	✿					
Heuchera sanguinea				✿	✿	✿						
Hosta				✿	✿	✿	✿					
Kniphofia				✿	✿	✿	✿	✿				
Leucanthemum				✿	✿	✿	✿					
Ligularia					✿	✿						

PLANT NAME	SPRING			SUMMER			AUTUMN			WINTER		
	EARLY	MID	LATE	EARLY	MID	LATE	EARLY	MID	LATE	EARLY	MID	LATE
Limonium latifolium						✿	✿					
Liriope muscari							✿	✿	✿			
Lobelia cardinalis					✿	✿	✿					
Lupinus polyphyllus				✿	✿							
Lychnis coronaria					✿	✿	✿					
Lysimachia punctata				✿	✿	✿						
Macleaya cordata					✿	✿						
Meconopsis				✿	✿	✿	✿					
Melianthus major				✿	✿	✿						
Mimulus			✿	✿	✿	✿						
Miscanthus sinensis						✿	✿	✿				
Monarda didyma					✿	✿						
Oenothera			✿	✿	✿	✿						
Paeonia				✿								
Papaver orientale			✿	✿	✿							
Penstemon				✿	✿	✿	✿	✿				
Phlox paniculata					✿	✿	✿					
Physostegia virginiana					✿	✿	✿					
Platycodon						✿	✿					
Polygonatum			✿									
Potentilla				✿	✿	✿	✿					
Primula vulgaris	✿											
Primula candelabra		✿	✿									
Pulmonaria	✿	✿	✿									
Pulsatilla vulgaris		✿	✿	✿								
Ranunculus			✿	✿	✿							
Rodgersia					✿	✿						
Romneya coulteri				✿	✿	✿						
Rudbeckia					✿	✿	✿	✿				
Salvia				✿	✿	✿	✿	✿				
Scabiosa				✿	✿	✿	✿					
Sedum spectabile						✿	✿					
Sisyrinchium striatum				✿	✿							
Solidago					✿	✿						
Stachys byzantina				✿	✿	✿	✿					
Stokesia laevis					✿	✿	✿					
Thalictrum				✿	✿							
Tiarella			✿	✿	✿							
Tradescantia virginiana				✿	✿	✿	✿					
Trillium		✿	✿	✿								
Verbascum				✿	✿	✿						
Viola odorata	✿	✿	✿									

INDEX

Published by Merehurst Limited, 1998
Ferry House, 51-57 Lacy Road, Putney, London SW15 1PR

Text copyright © Merehurst Limited
Photography copyright © Murdoch Books (except those listed below)

ISBN S407/1-85391-684-6

A catalogue of this book is available from the British Library.

SERIES EDITOR: Graham Strong

EDITOR: R. L. Rosenfeld

TEXT: Margaret Hanks

ILLUSTRATIONS: Sonya Naumov

DESIGNERS: Karen Awadzi and Jackie Richards

MANAGING EDITOR: Christine Eslick

COMMISSIONING EDITOR: Helen Griffin

PUBLISHER: Anne Wilson

PHOTOGRAPHS: All photographs by Lorna Rose except those by Margaret Hanks p 85 (L);
Graham Strong pp 2, 14, 28, 31 (R), 42, 79 (L), 91, 93 (R), 95 (R);
Eric Sawford pp 44, 57 (L), 63, 69, 95 (L), 98 (L), 105;
Pat Brindley pp 53, 64 (L and R), 70, 94, 96 (L), 98 (L);
Michael Warren pp 103 (L and R).

FRONT COVER: Red lupins
TITLE PAGE: Winter rose (Helleborus foetidus)